THE DAYS PLANNED FOR ME

A memoir of miraculous healing, devastating loss and learning to trust God

JEAN P. SULLIVAN

Jean P. Sullivan

Copywrite 2022 by Jean P. Sullivan

Unless otherwise indicated, all Scripture quotations are from the New King James Version®. Copywrite ©1982 by Thomas Nelson. Used by permission. All rights reserved.

Bible quotations marked NCV are from the New Century Version®. Copywrite © 2005 by Thomas Nelson. Used by permission. All rights reserved.

Ordering information:
For details, contact jean@jeanpsullivan.com

Print ISBN: 978-1-66785-978-1
eBook ISBN: 978-1-66785-979-8

Disclaimer

In writing this story I've been faithful to my memory and my journals, how-
ever, to protect the privacy of some individuals I have changed a few names.
And although details or events in this story may be recalled differently by
others, it is my hope and prayer that the message of God's loving, sovereign
providence amid difficult circumstances shines through. In addition, none of
the information presented in this book is intended to diagnose or treat any ill-
ness of, or relating to, what is discussed in this book. Always consult your own
physician before taking any medical action

ACKNOWLEDGEMENTS

No book is a solo enterprise, and this one came to be with the help and encouragement of many people over, ahem, many years. To Almeda Sullivan and Vicki Dinneen, who kept asking me how I was doing on a manuscript which sat collecting dust inside my computer, thank you for prodding me into publishing. To Peter, Stephanie and Jack Sullivan, Rebecca Markham, and Marilyn Morton who survived reading the first draft, thank you for your grace-filled ideas and input. Thank you, Leanne Sype, for your expert hacking, rearranging, and smoothing. Also thanks to beta readers Barbi Griffith, Gretchen Hanna and Shelly Weiser, and editor, Judy Couchman, who chiseled off a few more edges. And thank you for your wisdom, input, guidance and edits, Janice Osborne. I am also indebted to Stephanie Sullivan for her creativity in creating the design concept for my book cover even when she was eyeball-deep in caring for a newborn. And to my husband, Bill, who wakes up in the morning with the singular goal to encourage me in my writing and anything else I find to do, thank you. Finally, I thank Jesus, who walked us through the valley of the shadow of death more than once, our faithful and true Redeemer.

We will not hide them from their children, telling to the generation to come the praises of the LORD, and His strength and His wonderful works that He has done.

Psalm 78:4

For Annie

TABLE OF CONTENTS

PART 3: INTERPRETING THE STORY

PART 1:

THE VOW

INTRODUCTION

"Welcome!" the funeral director said. "Bill? Jean? Come in, come in! Good to meet you both. Can I get you anything—water, coffee?"

"I think we're fine, thanks," I said. Bill followed me into the mortuary office, steadying himself with his cane and sat down; I took a chair beside him. The three of us glanced at each other across the table, as if agreeing in an unspoken pact that our casket shopping excursion was an ordinary activity, like buying your first house...or last, as it were. Bill was there under duress—I insisted we do this ahead of time. "Pre-need" is what they call it in the business. Checking "Bill's final arrangements" off my list helped me bury the thought of losing him to the back of my mind.

The office's gold walls, maple bookshelves, and heavy brocade drapes had a warm glow to them. *Almost like a preview of heaven*, I thought. The wall of windows framed an expanse of lawn outside, lined with row upon row of perfectly spaced rectangular indentations. I knew one marked the grave of the infant son of one of my close friends. It occurred to me that she and I might come here together someday to visit her baby's grave ... and Bill's.

Losing Bill is going to be awful, but losing a child must be even worse, I rationalized to myself, as if grading the severity of a loss is even possible. But if my friend's loss was worse, then I figured, mine wasn't so bad. And besides, when an adult dies, we imagine them able to find their way on the other side. But when a child dies, who helps them find their way when they get there? Who takes care of them then?

The director interrupted my thoughts, opened a brochure, and described the relative merits of one burial plot over another. "Now this one has a beautiful old oak tree overlooking the gravesite, more private, and quite scenic."

I interrupted him. "We're really not here to buy real estate; we just want to get all the plans in writing."

"Oh, yes, of course," he cleared his throat. "We can certainly do that..."

Bill stared down at the brochure while I talked with the director.

"Good. We...*I* want to be able to just call someone and have everything taken care of when the time comes."

After about an hour of filling out forms and enduring the requisite golf cart tour around the cemetery, we got the plan in writing and promised we'd decide on a specific plot later. Bill and I walked out into the gray drizzle, and I helped him into the van.

"You owe me big time," he said under his breath.

"I promise I'll never make you go there again in your whole life."

"You know, Jean, I don't care where you bury me. It's not like I'm going to be looking around at the topiary. Just bury me in the backyard deep enough so the dog doesn't dig me up."

Gallows humor was always our M.O. to mask the sharp edges of our pain. I gave Bill a compulsory grin and drove out through the black wrought iron gate, relieved to have all his arrangements completed. My to-do list was the one thing I could control in a situation that was increasingly becoming out of control.

Chapter 1 :

IN THE BEGINNING

Bill and I met at work in 1978. He was a part-time college student and designed office space for a property management company in Orange, California. I was the receptionist. On his first day of work, Bill leaned his tall, lanky frame over my desk, furrowed his brow and asked, "Do you know where I can find some rubber bands?" Not one of the top pick-up lines I'd heard but memorable, nonetheless. His blond surfer hair, freckles and blue eyes were noted, but I decided he wasn't my type. I was looking for a Christian to date—at least that's what I frequently reminded myself—and I discovered after a few conversations with Bill that spiritual matters weren't exactly on the top of his radar. Or so it appeared. Truth was, I knew the same could be said of me.

Bill's dry humor was a draw, though, and it wasn't long before he regaled the rest of the office staff with the wit he concealed under his worried frown. My coworker Denise, Bill and I went out occasionally after work, the three of us, and whoever else wanted to join in. I don't remember exactly all the places we went. I recall urban cowboy clubs may have been one of the destinations. Bill had his own social life, too, and after about a year he met and married a young woman he knew from college. And a year after that, he left our company to design piping systems at an energy construction firm. The same weekend he started his new job, his wife up and left him. He called me at work to report his sad news.

"Jean? It's Bill."

"Oh, hi—how's your new job?"

"Okay..."

"Great—so what's up?"

"Debbie left me this weekend."

"What? You're kidding..."

"No, she said she found somebody else."

"Wow. I'm so sorry, Bill. I don't know what to say ..." I distinctly remember thinking, *what could she possibly think is wrong in less than a year of marriage??*

In that conversation, though, I thought to myself that the only thing that would bring Bill comfort was knowing that God loved him even if his wife didn't. He needed God to help him make sense of such a sudden loss. I, of course, knew everything he needed, but didn't have a thimble full of wisdom for my own life. At the time, I was living a hypocritical lifestyle, like a chameleon, fitting in with whatever crowd I happened to be with. In fact, after Bill's wife left him and he was looking for a roommate, I thought it would be a great idea to rent an apartment together.

My mother, however, thought I was nuts. "I don't think you guys living together is a good witness." 'Witness' being the Christian code word for example.

"Oh, we're just friends," I argued, which was the truth. I had my boyfriend and Bill had his ... cigarettes and pizza rolls. So, we moved in together against my mother's, and my, better judgment.

Oddly enough, things didn't go so well. When Bill wasn't at work, he sat in his rocker, staring at the TV while filling up his ashtray and rocking depressions into the carpet. After a couple of months, I couldn't stand living in his dark place, and he was done with my attempts to fix his problems, so we parted ways. My mother admitted she felt a tiny bit guilty when that happened. "You know, when I started praying, you guys stopped getting along and the next thing you know you weren't living together anymore," she admitted. *No kidding*, I thought.

Cigarettes and pizza rolls didn't provide much comfort for Bill, so he occasionally checked out the Saturday night concerts at Calvary Chapel in Costa Mesa. It was free entertainment, the girls were pretty, and he really didn't have much else to do he told me later. Each weekend after the band was done, Pastor Greg Laurie preached about Jesus. In his forthright style, he seemed to be speaking right to Bill about a Savior who loved him, died for his sins, and who would never leave him. This penetrated Bill's heart but not enough to convince him to dive into the whole Christianity gig with both feet. Up to that point, Christians were people Bill made fun of, he wasn't interested in actually becoming one.

Around this time Bill sent me a letter declaring his love for me. I was naively taken aback. *Weren't we just friends?* I thought. *What if he was rebounding too quickly after his divorce?* Then there was the question about his relationship to Jesus, the relationship he didn't have. I didn't have many lines in the sand but that was one of them. I told him no thanks, let's just continue being friends.

A few months later God had an appointment with Bill at the corner of Warner and Goldenwest in Huntington Beach. One morning on the way to work in his '78 silver Camaro, Bill accidentally ran a red light. He was driving east toward the sunrise and didn't see the light turn. He flew brake-less into the middle of the intersection as the driver's eyes in the Volkswagen bus he was about to T-bone grew as big as saucers. With no seatbelt or airbags, Bill instinctively dove headfirst into the passenger side floor, watching his sunglasses slide off his face in slow motion. His only thought: *It's too late. I'm a dead man on my way to hell.*

Miraculously, neither Bill nor the guy in the Volkswagen were hurt. However, it took a while for the fire department to get the "Jaws of Life" on-site to extract him from his accordioned car, so he had plenty of time to think. It was there inside his crumpled Camaro that he surrendered his life to Christ. When he called me a week later to tell me of his crash and subsequent conversion, it suddenly occurred to me that Bill was quite interesting and most eligible with a marvelous sense of humor. We made plans to get together to discuss the inherent risks of running red lights and God's mercy in providing escapes from death.

The next month, I was to take a quick trip to my sister's in the Bay Area to pick up my niece. Bill was familiar with San Francisco, and since I had never been there before, I asked him if he would like to go with me. He thought that was a great idea, so we headed north on I-5, over the mountains and into the farming communities of the Central Valley. I nonchalantly popped in a cassette tape subtly entitled "Marriage," and we listened as the pastor described biblical marriage 101. This wasn't entirely unusual, as Bill and I often talked about relationships. Only up to that point the discussions just involved his girlfriends or my boyfriends. At the time, Bill was dating another girl—we'll call her Linda—who took him to a little Baptist church where he served in their bus ministry. After we arrived in San Francisco and were seated at a cozy seafood restaurant on the pier, Bill threw out a little bait, "So what do you think...do you think I should I marry Linda?"

"Of course not."

Bill put his fork down. "Why not?"

"Well, why would you want to marry her, when you've got *me?*"

Bill looked up from his Shrimp Louie salad, "What do you mean by that?"

"Remember that letter you sent me a few months ago? Well, I feel that way, too, now."

Fortunately, Bill's affections for me weren't diminished, (and yes, he politely excused himself from his friendship with Linda), and a few months later we took the fast track to the church prayer chapel, promising ourselves to one another in front of God and the same pastor we listened to on the way to San Francisco. Surrounded by the love and hope-filled support of our families on that sweltering day in late summer, we vowed to be faithful to one another for better or worse, and in sickness and in health.

Wedding vows are a romantic notion when they're theoretical, like on your wedding day. The reality is we had no clue, none whatsoever, what we were getting ourselves into. What couple ever does? Ah, the wisdom of God in shielding us from knowing the hardships to come. Because when the pastor said, 'for better or worse,' what he really meant was worse. And when he said, 'in sickness and in health,' what he was really talking about was sickness.

Chapter 2:

LEARNING TO TRUST

Married life was challenging at the Sullivan house, as it is in all young married households. The challenges for us included having no money. And then there were the kids. Lots of kids. They were everywhere. Bill and I didn't plan on having a slew of kids. We just had them one at a time. Repeatedly. Our first son, Taylor, was born the first year. He was an easy, content baby, and because I couldn't bear to leave him in daycare and go back to work, I quit my lucrative secretarial career and became a stay-at-home mom. We pushed against the prevailing cultural tide in our roles; I reveled in my maternal domesticity, and Bill, in his role as chief hunter-gatherer. Bill's name means "determined guardian," and for some odd reason he took that to mean that he should, in fact, be the determined guardian.

Soon our family included a second son, Peter. We lived in a little town-house in Orange County listening to the sound of Disneyland's fireworks which could be heard at night after we put the kids to bed. Bill worked for a subsidiary of a petroleum company, where he helped develop a system to extract methane from deep inside of coal mines to convert it to natural gas. He frequently traveled to all points along the Appalachian Mountains, spending most of his time near a coal mine close to Birmingham, Alabama. Unfortunately, his company didn't want to commit to moving our little tribe to Alabama, so the kids and I stayed back in California and waited to see if the methane venture would turn into a permanent job. Not surprisingly, living apart for weeks at a time wore heavily on both Bill and me, not to mention the boys who missed their daddy terribly.

In April of 1986, Bill decided to take the proverbial bull by the horns and asked if I'd be willing to move to Alabama so we could be together again. The plan was to keep our townhouse in California, just in case things didn't work out in Alabama with his job. I thought it was a fine idea, but I was torn. Moving across country wasn't the problem, moving away from my mother was. Mom recently had been diagnosed with an aggressive type of leukemia. The doctors warned us in early January of that year that she likely had six months to live, at best. Although she was a nurse, she was reluctant to believe them because, you know, denial is a real thing. *If she could still work, it couldn't be that bad, could it?* But by the end of February her dwindling strength could no longer support her desire to work, and she resigned her job at the hospital. She moved in with my sister, Rebecca, and shifted into task mode, checking off projects under the heading "getting her affairs in order."

Anna Grace, (a name she despised, but I loved) was born in 1930 at the beginning of the Great Depression. She never had much in the way of earthly treasures, but after her diagnosis and on a day when she wasn't in denial, she sat down at the table and wrote out her will on a yellow legal pad, determining which of her belongings went to each of her children. Her Bible went to my sister, Susan, the oldest. The mid-century blond maple bedroom suite she and dad bought went to Rebecca. Marilyn got her thick, green cookbook that had pages stuck together with smudges of Christmas carrot pudding. I got Mom's wedding ring, whose sentimental value lay not in the broken marriage it represented but in the courage of the woman who wore it. One day in March she called me on the phone and asked if I'd go with her to the mortuary to pick out a casket. "Of course," I said, swallowing hard.

We walked into the mortuary office where a bespectacled mortician led the way to a room filled with all kinds of expensive caskets: mahogany caskets, gold-trimmed caskets, wood caskets, steel caskets. What motivates someone to get into the burying business I'll never know. But they seem to be uniquely skilled at selling caskets that your dead body will shortly reside in, much the same way they'd rent you a car if you were on your way to visit Cleveland: "Would you like to upgrade from a compact to a sedan? How about an SUV?" Mom walked past the SUV caskets to the back corner where she spotted an inexpensive, gray flannel-covered cardboard casket. "This one will be fine," Mom said, running her hand along the top of it. We followed the mortician back into his office and sat down as he assembled the pertinent forms on the desk in front of him. I gripped the handles of the chair as my throat tightened. The reality of what we were doing suddenly caught up with me. Mom was 56. I was 27. *This end-of-life stuff wasn't supposed to be happening at her age, was it? Shouldn't she be living until at least 85, like her mother did?*

The mortician interrupted my thoughts. "Do you have a minister you'd like to officiate..." he trailed off, looking up at Mom.

"I'd like our Pastor Romaine to do my service—he'll give a clear gospel message," she said.

"Oh yes, I know Romaine. He'll give it to them straight," the mortician winked. "We also have an organist...do you have any special hymns or music you'd like her to play?"

"Yes, "Wonderful Grace of Jesus." I want them marching out of there at the end."

Not sure what that was all about, but the mortician carefully wrote down all her instructions and then carried his orders, and eventually her, out with aplomb.

Driving back home after our pre-planning meeting, Mom asked me to sew a blouse for her to wear in the casket—"pink with pearl buttons, please."

"Sure thing," I gulped.

She then switched gears and brought up the possibility of my move back to Alabama to be with Bill. "What do you think I should do?" I asked. "I want to be with Bill, but I don't want to leave … you. Not now."

"Well, you know what your Bible says: the two shall become one. You guys need to be together." Her unselfish, wise words were right, but I was conflicted. None of us knew what Mom's timeline was, but if I went to Alabama, this might be the last time I'd see her. I parked the car in front of Rebecca's condo and came around to help Mom out. Wrapping my arms around her weakened body, I hugged her tight while we both cried.

"Why, why, why?" I railed at God all the way home. My head rested against the car window, and I struggled to see the freeway in front of me. Mom was right. I needed to be with Bill, but the thought of never seeing her again turned my heart inside out.

Soon, Bill flew out from Alabama to California, and we packed up Taylor and Peter and drove back east along the southern route through Texas, Louisiana, Mississippi and finally to a tiny, humble apartment Bill rented in a small town outside of Birmingham. We were there just one month when Mom's doctors announced there was just a short window of time to try one last dose of big-gun chemo. They warned us in not-so-diplomatic medicalese that it would either cure her…or kill her. Not surprisingly, my resolve to be in Alabama with Bill flew out the window as soon as I heard that news. And, of course, Bill mercifully sent me home to California to walk through these last few weeks with Mom. Each day I drove back and forth between our townhouse and the hospital, taking my turn sitting with Mom as she slowly declined. Mom's hair was gone, her waxy skin was pale, and the excruciating sores in her mouth only allowed for tiny sips of water. On a Tuesday morning in late June the doctors called a family conference and confirmed to us what we suspected; the chemo had failed. Mom had hours, maybe days, left. My brothers, sisters and I set up a vigil schedule so someone could be by her bedside to the end. Sitting there beside her on my watch, listening to her uneven breathing, it seemed that the only thing recognizable on her body were her hands.

My mind drifted back to a humid summer evening twenty years before when these same hands opened her old, black leather Bible to Psalm 91. Back and forth we swayed on a rusty, aqua-green glider, as Mom helped me memorize each verse. I repeated them over and over to her, while the cicadas chorused in response: "He who dwells in the secret place of the Most High shall abide under the shadow of the Almighty. I will say of the Lord, "*He is my refuge and my fortress; My God, in Him I will trust.*"[1]

Years before, Mom waitressed for many years to support her family. And before going back to school to become a nurse, these same hands that lay motionless on the crisp hospital sheets once emptied her pockets of one-dollar bills, arranging them carefully onto her bedroom dresser after working at the restaurant each night. Dad left when I was 8, and with his income gone, those dollars from her tips stretched around rent, groceries, and school clothes. Mom didn't overtly teach any of us fiscal responsibility; she modeled it.

Eventually, her hands wrote reports, took tests, and learned to place IVs. She persisted in her studies, finally earning her RN degree at the age of 54. And before she died, her hands hugged all her children and grandchildren close, loving each of us the most and the best.

Mom died early on Saturday morning, June 28, 1986. On my way back to the hospital to meet with my siblings, I drove along the 91 freeway as the brilliant orange, purple and blue colors of the sunrise painted the sky. *God is still in control*, I thought. *He still commands the sun to rise each day.* A verse came to mind, "My grace is sufficient for you, for My strength is made

---

1   Psalm 91:1-2 (NKJ).

perfect in weakness."[2] His grace was enough for me that morning. I knew beyond a shadow of a doubt that Mom's last breath on earth was followed by her first breath in heaven.

After her funeral, we gathered at Rebecca's place to divide the remaining keepsakes Mom left behind: a few nurse's hats and pins, a name tag from the last hospital she worked at, and four framed bird prints, all laid out on her bed. We took turns choosing the mementos that meant something to us. I settled on two of the bird pictures, reminiscent of James Audubon prints with the Latin names of each bird; one picture was primarily blue, the other yellow, her favorite color. The prints reminded me of the chickadees, finches and cardinals outside our little house tucked into the Western Pennsylvania woods. Mom never put curtains up on our kitchen windows, so she could enjoy an unobscured view of her feathered friends flitting from branch to branch. At least that's why I thought we never had curtains. It didn't occur to me that maybe we couldn't afford them. I took the bird prints and hung them on my wall to remind me of her.

That next year after Mom died, I felt God's presence wrapping me like a warm, comforting blanket. I knew she was completely healed in heaven. Yet that didn't erase the emptiness of life without her. I missed hearing her voice, her laugh, her encouragement, her humor. I missed her all the time, really, but never more so than when each new Sullivan baby squalled into this world without her arms to greet them.

---

2   2 Corinthians 12:9.

Chapter 3 :

EARLY MINISTRY

By 1993 we had five sons: Taylor, Peter, Andy, David, and Jack. We moved to Washington to be closer to Bill's family, and eventually bought a split-level house in Tacoma. On our first weekend there, we visited a church that immediately felt like home. We soon got involved with different ministries, made friends, and settled in. By then Bill was working in middle management for an environmental engineering company, which included traveling to Hawaii at least 30% of the time. Although ocean breezes were a welcome respite for him from the gray drizzle of the Pacific Northwest, we both disliked the challenge it was for him to stay connected to our growing family.

One hot Sunday in August, we walked outside after the church service and stood beneath the shade of the porte-cochere. Little did we know that Bill's career trajectory was about to take a 180° turn. The pastor greeted us and after covering the usual pleasantries, he pulled Bill aside to talk. The kids were antsy after being in their Sunday School classes, so I walked them over to our van and lifted three-month-old Jack into his car seat while the older ones piled in behind. We rolled down the windows and waited while Bill

nt infant. Bill felt totally inadequate, having had no formal training
ved church members. It was all on-the-job.

couple of hours later I heard his truck pull into our driveway. Bill
up the stairs, slumped down at the kitchen table and said, "I've never
f like that..." his voice catching. "*What do you say to that pain?* What
possibly say or do to comfort them?" He leaned back into his chair
ed at the ceiling, oblivious to the wet streaks running down his face.

he funeral service was a few days later and the pastor came back to
at the gravesite service. A small gathering of friends and family stood
he shade of an awning sheltering the tiny casket. I felt almost like
sive witness to the loss of the young parents, as their shoulders were
th an almost visible burden of inconsolable grief.

ll the church ladies brought the family meals for a few weeks after-
roviding food seems like an insignificant thing to do in the face of
nonumental loss, but of course that's what you do. What else could
? Those of us who never suffered the loss of a child could only try to
, try to be compassionate. As I visited with the young mother in her
one afternoon a few weeks later, it dawned on me that losing a child
league beyond anything I knew, even compared with the death of
her. I tried to say the right things, but to be honest, I didn't *want* to
mprehend what she was feeling. I hoped just sitting there with her
ehow helpful. I discovered much later that often the quiet presence
nd is infinitely more comforting than any words they might say.

ife plodded on as it does, and our church continued to grow as did
ily. Soon we were expecting our sixth child. I seem to recall that by the
had our fifth, people quit rolling their eyes at us. Most of the time.
my friends, another mother of five kids, told me that her husband
ld her, "We can have as many children as we want, and it's no one's
s but ours." *That's right*, I thought. *Why should I feel embarrassed about
ny kids we have?* His comment emboldened me, and both Bill and I
if you will, to continue to leave that proverbial barn door open. We

and the pastor finished their conversation. After a fev

over to the van and got in.

"You're not going to believe this," looking in th

he backed out of the parking lot.

"What did he want to talk to you about?"

"He asked me if I would consider coming on st

tion pastor."

"You're kidding—really?"

"I don't know where he got that idea. I could n

"I can see you doing that," I said. "…would you

grocery store before we go home?"

Bill headed toward the store, pulled into a par

the engine and stared down at the steering wheel.

"You have administrative gifts and the church i

you," I reasoned.

Bill gave me a sideways glance.

"Maybe God is calling you to it?"

Bill opened the door and got out. "Yeah, mayb

A few months later, Bill decided to jump in. H

trips to Hawaii and the office with a view of Lake Wa

occupational ministry. His initial experiences worki

the proverbial trial by fire. Ministry was a different w

There were no deliverables, no sales quotas, and no ol

success. Just people's spiritual lives and eternities. No

The pastor went on vacation as soon Bill cam

job to field any congregational emergencies in the p

immediately, he got a call to go to the hospital to b

whose baby had died at birth. Bill got into his truck,

and walked into a room where a grieving mother sa

believed, as the Bible says, that each of our children are blessings. Number six Sullivan was no exception. But I soon was reminded that being pregnant was no guarantee that a healthy baby would be born at the end of nine months.

When I was about four months pregnant, Bill and I walked through the local mall with the kids when I suddenly noticed some cramping and chills. I looked around for the nearest bench. "Can we sit down for a minute?"

Bill looked at me, frowning with concern. "What's the matter?"

"I-I'm feeling crampy—"

He put his arm around my shoulders. "Should we go home?"

"Yeah...I really don't feel well." We slowly walked back to the van, climbed in, and drove home. I went upstairs to our bedroom and laid down for a nap. When I woke up, I was bleeding. A lot.

"Bill—*Bill!*" I yelled from our bathroom. He ran in, helped me gather some things and we broke speed laws on our way to the hospital, where the emergency room doctor ordered an ultrasound. My sister, Rebecca, who lived nearby, met us there.

The doctor came into the exam room with an ultrasound picture in her hand. "The baby looks good, but you have a significant tear in the placenta. You can see it here…"

She pointed at the ultrasound picture. "I'm afraid you'll probably lose the pregnancy," she said matter-of-factly.

After the doctor left the room, Rebecca looked up at me, "So what do you want to do?"

"Pray," was my immediate response. Right then Bill, Rebecca, and I closed our eyes and pleaded with God to spare this precious life still somersaulting inside my belly.

Back home, I faithfully followed the doctor's instructions not to get up for anything but to go to the bathroom. The next day my friend, Jane, stopped by the house after church to see me. She walked into my room and sat down on the edge of the bed.

"How are you doing, girl?"

"Not so good, I guess…just trying to follow doctor's orders. You're praying, right?"

She reached over and put her hand on mine. "Yes, ma'am, and everyone at church prayed hard for you guys this morning."

Years before, Jane had lost a baby girl, only a few weeks old. However, I didn't immediately connect the dots between her loss and my current crisis. It was much later when I considered how selfless she was to draw near to the pain she was all too familiar with.

After a few weeks I was still horizontal, and miraculously, the pregnancy was holding. The doctor ordered another ultrasound to see how things were going, and as Bill watched the screen, the tech showed us how the placental tear was healing. He called out the details of the scan: "Here's the heart—looking good. Four chambers ... and let's see if it'll cooperate with us to determine…"

"It's a girl!" Bill confidently announced.

"Good call, Dad," the tech grinned.

Bill's eyes filled with tears. "Yep, I've seen lots of boy ultrasounds, and that doesn't look like any of those!"

I just laid there watching, listening, laughing, and crying. *Thank you, Lord, so much, for sparing her life.*

At the beginning of May, we welcomed little Olivia to our family. And my friend Jane was one of the first to hold Olivia when we brought her home.

Sullivan life hummed along and by 1997 our six kids ranged in age from two to fifteen. Between unending loads of laundry and trips to Costco, I chased the kids around to baseball practices and youth group activities while Bill oversaw the business of a growing church.

One morning I followed Bill up the stairs from the laundry room and noticed his left foot dragging across the edge of each step as he walked up. When he reached the top, he swung his left leg around, unable to lift it in front of him. He sat down on the wingback chair in the living room and looked over at me.

"I think I need a cane." He looked down at his leg. "My leg is getting weak. Maybe from that useless back surgery?"

Bill suffered chronic back pain from a work injury in the early '80s and had surgery in 1996. We wondered if the leg weakness might be a recurrence of those problems. Fortunately, Dr. Stewart, our general practitioner, had an uncanny ability to diagnose any kind of ailment. And if he couldn't figure it out, he'd send us to someone who could.

"Should I make an appointment with Dr. Stewart?" I asked.

"Yeah," Bill said, which relieved and worried me at the same time. Usually, he avoided doctors. For him to be willing to go to the doctor indicated to me that he was as concerned as I was.

Dr. Stewart ordered tests that came back with inconclusive results. Leaving no stone unturned, he sent us to the University of Washington Medical Center for more tests. A few weeks later, we met him to go over the results. He walked into the exam room with Bill's file and sat down. "They think you might have MS—Multiple Sclerosis. But they're not sure..." Dr. Stewart glanced up at us, cleared his throat, and then shuffled the papers in front of him. "...so, we don't need to think about that yet. Let's not think about MS right now. We need to monitor your symptoms for a while before we'll know for sure. But let's not even think about MS yet."

Dr. Stewart kept analyzing Bill's file, looking up at us and then down at the test results in front of him. *MS sounds bad, but at least it isn't fatal like leukemia or some sort of cancer,* I thought. It's true that MS has its own challenges, yet for some reason, I thought MS would at least be manageable.

Since the doctors couldn't pinpoint a diagnosis, Bill decided that a cane would solve most of his immediate problems. So, he bought one and went back to his comfort zone: work. Work was where the attention was on other people and *their* problems; work was where he could forget about his own.

Chapter 4:

SHADOWS OF
THINGS TO COME

Our family vacations usually involved tents, porta potties and bucket loads of DEET. Nothing about camping spelled rest and relaxation to me; the Marriott would've been my preferred choice. But I was overruled by our kids who liked to ignite marshmallows over a crackling fire, and Bill, whose childhood memories of tent camping conveniently didn't include his aching back. And then there was our checkbook, which typically ran lean. So, tent camping it was. We packed up Bill's '69 Chevy truck with the hand-me-down tent from his sister, the '50's-era army green gas stove from his parents, and a cooler full of hot dogs, canned chili and whatever other genetically modified kid-friendly food we could find. I surreptitiously hid the s'mores supplies in the diaper bag, the kids piled into the van and off we'd go. After we arrived at the scenic campground crowded with a quarter of the population of the county, it took me all of about seven minutes to plot my escape.

One time we went camping it was Olivia who saved the day. When she was about a year old, she woke up in the middle of the night vomiting all over her blanket, pajamas and anything within a three-foot radius of her playpen. Another time, it was the weather. The clouds split open in the middle of the night, and we were flash-flooded out of our tent. By the summer of 1998, though, neither Bill nor I were much in the mood to rough it, so we took the kids to a cabin in the Cascade mountains. It was a cedar A-frame with a cozy kitchen, a screen door that kept bugs out, a big front porch and enough space for everyone to have their own bed. Not the Marriott, but definitely a few steps up from our old tent.

In front of our cabin facing west lay a spacious green lawn, perfect for playing catch with the boys. After throwing the ball back and forth a few times with them the first evening, Bill ambled up to the porch and sat down in the Adirondack chair beside me.

"My arm feels weak," he whispered, out of earshot of the kids.

"That's weird, what do you think it is?"

"I don't know. I can't even catch the ball, much less throw it." He bit his lip and looked out toward the boys playing in the shadows of the setting sun. Bill seemed distant the rest of our time there, no doubt wondering why his body was failing him so rapidly. We had gone to the doctor. MS wasn't confirmed, but his symptoms seemed to be getting worse. I could feel a baseball-sized knot taking up residence in my stomach.

A few months later I sat down to read my Bible one night and came across a verse in the Old Testament book of Jeremiah. "'For I will restore health to you and heal you of your wounds,' says the LORD, 'Because they called you an outcast, *saying:* "This *is* Zion; No one seeks her."'[3] I read it over and over for a long time. The passage describes how Israel was carried away captive to Babylon, and that God promised to restore them and heal their nation. The verse seemed to jump out at me, and a thought crossed my mind, *what if God would restore health to Bill like He promised to do for Israel?* I didn't

---

3   Jeremiah 30:17.

want to be guilty of manipulating verses to suit my own situation yet felt the Holy Spirit somehow speaking to me that this verse might apply to Bill, too. Maybe God wanted me to ask that He *would* heal Bill. I didn't really know. It hadn't occurred to me to ask God to heal him because who was ever healed from diseases like MS? I wrote the date, "October 3, 1998," beside the verse in my Bible and decided that night to begin to pray specifically for Bill's healing.

Back then, I don't remember feeling afraid or worried as much as simply curious as to what God was doing in our lives. Since Bill was able to work, things—at least to this point—went along normally, occasionally interrupted by doctor's appointments. Unbeknownst to us though, Bill's health was about to spiral down.

The next month at a friend's wedding, the bride and groom dismissed their guests row by row after the ceremony. When it was our turn to get up and leave, I leaned over to Bill and asked him how he was feeling. His reply sounded like his mouth was full of marbles. My stomach dropped and I immediately thought he was having a stroke. I discreetly guided him into the church office to try and figure out what was going on. The left side of his tongue was numb; nothing else seemed amiss. But why? What was going on with his body?

Fortunately, it wasn't a stroke, although now I can't recall which doctor drew that conclusion. Yet the numbness remained, and Bill compensated for the weakness in his tongue by carefully enunciating each word when he talked. Because his tongue was numb, eating also became problematic. Jack, who was about five at the time, remembers how quiet all the kids got around the dinner table when Bill choked on food. I tried to make the Heimlich Maneuver seem like an ordinary part of dinnertime, but somehow jumping up to unclog Dad's throat didn't lend itself to relaxing conversation. Bill resigned himself to eating soft foods, instant breakfast becoming his go-to menu item. Every time I'd go to Costco, I'd throw another can of instant breakfast into the cart. While Bill found his body to be quite frustrating and embarrassing, I just kept a stiff upper lip and did my best to keep the plates spinning.

However, my forced calm exterior for Bill and the kids sucked every ounce of energy I had. Inside, fear took a seat next to the knot in my stomach. I worked out a lot of anxiety by journaling and praying each night, but this train we were on seemed to be careening down the track with nothing in its way to stop it.

By January of 1999, we still didn't have a diagnosis when another troubling symptom presented itself. Walking up the stairs one day, Bill made it to the top while straining to catch his breath.

"What's the matter?" I asked. Bill sat down on the nearest chair.

"Can't breathe..." he whispered.

His symptoms so far had been halfway manageable, but this was beyond my expertise. Caregiving was taking a toll; I was fearful, stressed out, and exhausted from trying to keep a calm face for the kids and for Bill. I wasn't a nurse, and yet I was constantly making nursing decisions for him. Breathing was kind of important. People who don't breathe typically die. I just wished I knew what his diagnosis was so I would know what to do, and where all this was headed.

I called Dr. Stewart, and he asked me to bring Bill down to his office immediately. We rushed down to the office and after examining Bill, he sent us over to the hospital in town where Bill was admitted and quickly diagnosed with pneumonia. The doctors there also suspected he had ALS, or Lou Gehrig's disease. ALS has a life expectancy of about five years, less if the disease presents with "bulbar" symptoms, like breathing or speaking difficulty, which Bill had. They say God never gives peace before a crisis, but rather when you need it, and that was the case for us.

"I am filled with an overwhelming sense of God's presence in our situation—and also a sense that His plan is perfect and exciting. He is so amazing, so perfect, so loving. All (or one of the things) He wants of us is that we would

simply believe, and act in obedience to that faith in Him. And since my faith comes from Him in the first place, what He is asking shouldn't be that difficult of an exercise!" Journal, March 2, 1999

Having God's peace, however, didn't mean our problems magically disappeared. Bill's tests proved negative for ALS, which put us back to square one, a relief and frustration at the same time. One minute we had a diagnosis, the next we didn't.

After the pneumonia scare, Bill slowly recovered and went back to work, which was a huge relief to me. Work always was his comfort zone, yet even his sedentary job was becoming more and more uncomfortable. His whole left side seemed weaker each day, so he had a recliner put in his office to lie back on when he wasn't feeling well, which is not something most employers would agree to. The church made accommodations for Bill's physical needs as much as they could, yet as his health deteriorated, his ability to do his job declined with it. In retrospect, Bill should have resigned as executive pastor right then.

On good days, Bill went to work and tried to forget he was sick, and on bad days, he stayed in bed, too weak and in too much pain to get up. There seemed to be no answers, only questions. *How long? How bad? What can help?* I hoped that a diagnosis would clue us in as to what to expect and maybe point us in a direction that medicine or treatment could help. I spent hours searching the Internet for every motor-neuron-muscular disease I could find, then assembled the major symptoms, compared them with Bill's, and invariably ended up with more questions. Bill's illness was a puzzle I needed to figure out.

Always a pragmatist in my thoughts about what was happening, I remember thinking to myself, *People get sick...they get sick and sometimes they die. I guess this is our turn.* My experience with my mother's illness and death drove most of this thinking, I guess. Also, my oldest sister, Susan, was diagnosed with breast cancer around this time and died in September of 1999, leaving her husband and three older children to mourn. So subconsciously

I figured life-threatening illness happens to everyone. Worst case scenario, Bill will die, leave me a single mom with six kids, then I'll go to work and God will help us...somehow.

A psychologist friend once told me he thought I had an abnormal expectation that I would be left alone, as if I spent my life gearing up for it. I feigned offense, but it was the truth. Our family history includes many generations of households headed by women, beginning with my grandmother Alice Magee, whose first husband died when she was pregnant with her sixth child. He was injured when a piece of equipment from a train he was working on fell on his head and he died a few days later in the hospital. Too poor for life insurance and years before Social Security, Grandma Magee supported her brood partly by renting out rooms in her house.

The pattern continued when my dad left my mother with five kids to raise on her own. Thankfully, God and Mom's waitress jobs kept us clothed and fed and out of the welfare office. I felt my grandmother and mother were part of a cloud of witnesses reminding me that God would take care of us when Bill died; I just didn't know how.

One comfort for me was that because Bill believed in Jesus, I knew his eternity was secure. Even in my concern for our future, I knew at least he'd be fine. The verse describing life as a *vapor that appears for a little time and then vanishes away*[4] was a constant echo in my mind. I knew this from my experience with Mom. Life-threatening illnesses are often used by God to remind us that our time here on earth is short. I knew these things and had lived them. God's Word was my anchor against waves of uncertainty. So, I forced these thoughts to the front of my mind and pushed the fear of our future to the back of it.

---

4   James 4:14b.

Chapter 5:

DIAGNOSIS

n July of 1999, the church sent our family on a trip to Disneyland so we could make some happy memories with Bill. What better place to make memories than Disneyland, "The Happiest Place on Earth"? My brother, Dan, and his wife and kids joined us that day, so we enjoyed a bit of a family reunion too. There are downsides to Disneyland, however, besides the second mortgage required to just walk into the place. It covers an area roughly the size of Rhode Island and was yet another reminder to us of how much Bill's illness had progressed. He simply could not walk long distances anymore. The upside was Mickey rents out scooters for people who can't walk. So, 4-year-old Olivia, wearing a tall, purple princess hat with a flowing veil, perched on Bill's lap as he maneuvered the scooter around the park. We watched fireworks that night until, exhausted, we clambered onto Mufasa's tram that delivered us to the zip code where I had parked the van. Amazingly, Bill had the stamina to make it through the day. The scooter helped.

We also did a little sightseeing on our trip too, including watching cars speed down the freeway. Southern California's traffic is notoriously congested, and during one of our bumper-to-bumper adventures, Bill got car sick. He laid down in the back seat with his eyes closed for the remainder of the trip, and we added dizziness to his growing number of symptoms. Somehow, though, despite the dark cloud of why we were in California in the first place, our time there was a refreshing respite.

When we got home, we went back to see his neurologist. Bill's symptoms were leading him toward a diagnosis of a type of Parkinson's, but which one, he wasn't sure. I started researching Bill's symptoms and tried to match them up to the various types of Parkinson's. I came across information about Progressive Supranuclear Palsy, or PSP, which has the unusual visual symptom of an inability to direct eye movements. So, I decided to test Bill's eyes myself.

"Can you come over here so I can check something out, Bill?"

Bill reached for his cane, walked across the living room, and stood in front of me.

I faced him and watched his eyes. "Okay, look up," I said. Bill looked up toward the ceiling. "Now look down."

He could not do it. His eyes got halfway down and then made a right-hand turn. He could not make them look straight down. In addition, his eyes jiggled when he tried to focus, which made reading almost impossible. Fortunately, our ophthalmologist recommended that Bill be fitted with prisms in his eyeglass lenses to help with vertical eye movement. In October, we made another appointment with our neurologist who confirmed that Bill did indeed have Progressive Supranuclear Palsy.

Progressive Supranuclear Palsy, or PSP, is a more aggressive type of Parkinson's, usually presenting after the age of 60. There is no cure. Bill already had the symptoms of loss of balance, difficulty with speech and swallowing, and weakness and pain on his whole left side. He was also apathetic and flat in his facial expressions. He stopped initiating conversations and had trouble organizing his thoughts. The doctor cautioned us that based on the worsening symptoms, he estimated Bill's prognosis to be about two years, and at that time Bill was only 40 years old.

My reaction to his diagnosis was one of resignation. Calm, even. I knew a serious diagnosis was coming; Bill's symptoms greeted me every morning, so it wasn't a surprise when the doctor confirmed PSP. The roles in our marriage had already necessarily evolved into caregiver and patient.

Bill reluctantly gave me oversight of our finances. I even considered taking the car keys away from him when he told me he'd gotten lost while running an errand. He said he had to pull over to the side of the road because he forgot where he was. Fortunately, that experience was so unnerving to him that he made the decision himself to quit driving alone.

We were candid with our children about the seriousness of what was going on. When we had new information from the doctor, we'd tell them. Not surprisingly, each one of our children dealt with it in their own way. Our oldest, Taylor, was in his last year of high school by that time and decided to do his senior project on PSP. Bill and I wanted to support him, since parents were welcome to attend the presentations. Driving down to the school, we parked and picked up our visitor's tags at the office. I followed Bill into the classroom and sat down. After Taylor introduced his topic, the students glanced over at his dad holding his cane then grew silent and somber. They all listened while Taylor matter-of-factly described life at the Sullivan's:

Complications of Progressive Supranuclear Palsy result primarily from hindered muscle movements. These complications may include:

1.   Frequent falling, which can lead to head injuries, fractures, and other injuries.

2.   Difficulty focusing your eyes, which can also lead to injuries.

3.   Problems with reading, driving a car, or other tasks requiring hand-eye coordination.

4.   Difficulty sleeping.

5. Difficulty looking at bright lights.

6. Problems swallowing, which can lead to choking or inhaling food or liquid into your airway (aspiration). Aspiration can develop into pneumonia, which is the most common cause of death in people with Progressive Supranuclear Palsy.[5]

The teacher discreetly dabbed at her eyes. The students in the classroom stared down at their desks. On the way home Bill and I discussed that perhaps the topic of PSP was a little heavier than Taylor's class was expecting.

Peter, who was in tenth grade by then, worked out his frustrations in the backyard, pitching the ball into the backstop of our garden shed door. The reality was the shed was firewood from the day we moved in, but after Peter pitched into it, the door gave way and holes appeared between the splintered wood. Bill watched him from the sliding glass door overlooking the backyard, depressed that he couldn't throw the ball with his son and frustrated that the shed was falling apart. Peter was no doubt frustrated that his father's body was falling apart, too.

Andy and David stayed occupied with soccer. Friends of ours picked them up and took them to practice and the games because by that time Bill had stopped driving, and I was focused on my caregiving duties. Bill couldn't even go to most of their games because he'd get carsick. On the occasion he did need to go somewhere we always brought a big stainless-steel bowl in the van, just in case.

Jack and Olivia were about six and four-years-old at the time. Jack usually played quietly by himself, keeping the neighborhood safe from evil with his superhero action figures and plastic dinosaurs. Olivia took walks with her daddy when he felt up to it. Bill held Olivia's hand in his, and with his cane in the other hand they would slowly stroll over to the neighbor's farm, stopping to feed the horses blades of grass growing by the side of the road.

---

5   https://www.ninds.nih.gov/health-information/patient-caregiver-education/
     fact-sheets/progressive-supranuclear-palsy-fact-sheet#3281_7.

I prepared for the worst yet prayed constantly for God to heal Bill. One night a story from the Bible caught my attention when I read in Acts how the lame man was healed by the Apostle Peter. In the story, the religious leaders arrested Peter and the Apostle John because they'd healed a man by the power of Jesus, the target of their hatred and envy:

"Then Peter, filled with the Holy Spirit, said to them, "Rulers of the people and elders of Israel: If we this day are judged for a good deed *done* to a helpless man, by what means he has been made well, let it be known to you all, and to all the people of Israel, that by the name of Jesus Christ of Nazareth, whom you crucified, whom God raised from the dead, by Him this man stands here before you whole. This is the 'stone which was rejected by you builders, which has become the chief cornerstone.' Nor is there salvation in any other, for there is no other name under heaven given among men by which we must be saved."[6] Further in the story it describes that "the man was over forty years old on whom this miracle of healing had been performed."

I believe that the Bible is true. And I believed that God could heal Bill. And I knew that according to Romans 15:4, these verses weren't written only as a historical account of the early church, they were written so that we might have hope. And just as God healed this lame man, I knew God could heal Bill. I just prayed that He would.

---

6   Acts 4:8-12, 22.

Chapter 6:

OUTCAST

By late 1999, our church had a weekly attendance of about 1,200 people, and between the main campus and a few new ministry ventures, things were getting beyond Bill's capacity to manage. Yet he continued going to work. Bill took his responsibility as a husband, father, and provider as a solemn duty, as if it all depended on him, but his ability to work was slipping away. He was in continual pain, his cognitive function was slow, he had poor balance and vision. Nothing was working like it had before. His declining work performance was no doubt a frustration for the senior pastor, too, and on January 5, 2000, he called Bill into his office, relieved him of his duties and sent him home.

That night Bill and I sat in the living room after the kids had gone to bed and tried to wrap our heads around what had happened that day. We shouldn't have been surprised. The doctors told us his diagnosis was life-limiting, and we knew it was only a matter of time before Bill would have to quit working. But like the proverbial frog in the kettle, we had adjusted to living in a crisis mode that was occasionally interspersed with normalcy. However, it was unrealistic for us to assume our church could operate that way. They needed an executive pastor who was clicking on all eight cylinders, not just one or two. Bill was dismissed, and on the surface, that was it.

But underneath the loss of employment, God also brought something deeper to light. Bill's identity as "determined guardian" was off the table. Gone. His greatest fear, not having the ability to provide for his family, was now a crushing reality. Bill knew theoretically that God was our Provider, but in his heart, *he* had always been the one through whom God had provided. The idea that God could take care of his family without his help was hard to accept. He confided to me later that night, "It became crystal clear today why I got this disease. Because I refused to be humble, I am being humbled. That's what I learned in school today."

I appreciated Bill's transparency; however, his dismissal seemed abrupt to me. On one hand, I knew Bill needed to slow down. On the other hand, I didn't understand why he was suddenly sent home. *Couldn't he at least minister on a scaled back basis, like occasional counseling?* I wondered. Bill's neurologist had suggested as much in a note to the leadership of the church. In my mind, I thought he could at least do something to contribute to the ministry, if only to not feel so useless.

Within a month, however, Bill was informed that not only was he no longer needed on staff, but he was also not welcome to participate in *any* ministry. There seemed to be a growing suspicion of Bill for some reason. Dealing with his illness had been the focus of this trial to this point, but now he also felt a growing sense of rejection. No calls. No emails. No nothing. It was then that the second part of the verse I noted in 1998 started to make more sense to me.

"'For I will restore health to you and heal you of your wounds,' says the LORD, 'Because they called you an outcast *saying*: "This is Zion; No one seeks her."' [7]

---

7 Jeremiah 30:17.

My attention had been on the first part of the verse, that maybe, just *maybe,* God might restore Bill's health as He had restored the nation, Israel. The second part, *they called you an outcast,* I had overlooked. *How could we possibly feel like outcasts?* I thought back then. We had a church family with close relationships with both lay people and the leadership. Being an outcast isn't something either of us had experienced to that point. Yet after Bill was dismissed, he felt ostracized; we both did. The trial of his illness was compounded by this mysterious silence from the leadership. In fact, dealing with his illness was not nearly as emotionally painful because it wasn't caused by any one person. Now not only did we face the loss of Bill's health and job, but also the loss of his friends.

A few weeks later we went to a counselor to discuss Bill's illness and cascade of losses. Ironically, the one thing Bill despised more than having a terminal illness was talking about it. I, on the other hand, didn't mind ruminating on morose subjects, and looked forward to unloading on someone who would share our burdens, if only for an hour-long office visit.

The counselor listened while he acknowledged Bill's physical, relational and ministerial losses; Bill was suffering loss in every area of his life: his job, being involved with leadership decisions, playing with the kids, eating real food, breathing…little things like that. The counselor's advice? Rest in God's grace and quit looking "out there" for meaning in life. He zeroed in specifically on Bill's identity at work which had formerly been Bill's happy place.

Bill told me that before he got sick, much of his self-worth came from what others thought of him. He identified as a people-pleaser. He lived for "atta-boys" and affirmation, especially at work. It seemed that perhaps one of the purposes of God in this double trial of illness and conflict was to chip away at the veneers of Bill's identity so that he would be solely secure in Christ. Neither of us, however, could understand all the reasons why Bill's illness happened, but we believed that it was allowed by a sovereign God who permits suffering in our lives to change us into the image of Christ. *Painful?* Incredibly. *Worthwhile?* I wasn't there yet.

A book I read (and re-read!) during this time, *The Making of a Leader,* by Dr. J. Robert Clinton, describes what he calls a "crisis process item." "It refers to special intense pressure situations in life, used by God to test and to teach dependence on Him."[8] This is where we were. We were in the middle of a crisis process item, learning dependence on God. All other props to our identity, ego, and lives, had been kicked away. The counselor encouraged Bill to "Look inwardly at what God is speaking to you, and value what He is teaching you." Again, easier said than done.

As we stood to leave, the counselor recommended another book *When Life Hurts,* by Philip Yancey. I bought it that day and devoured it in a few hours. The last chapter describes how God encourages us not only through His Word and through His Holy Spirit, but also through the body of Christ, the church. I found this to be true, because as the leadership of the church pulled away from us, many lay people in the church drew near.

---

8   *The Making of a Leader,* by Dr. J. Robert Clinton, page 238.

Chapter 7:

THE VOW

M ost of the rank and file of the church were not aware of what was going on between the leadership and us. We didn't discuss it but with a handful of people, mostly friends and family from outside of the church. Thankfully, the relationships with our lay friends within the church strengthened during this time. In fact, our home bible study group had been trying to find ways to help us, but I hadn't known what to ask for. Formulating thoughts to communicate, *I need this or that*, required cohesive sentences and planning and prioritizing—more oars than I was rowing with at the time.

Our home group decided to quit waiting for me to come up with the plan and arranged for a woman to come over every other Tuesday to clean our house. A clean house cleaned the cobwebs out of my mind, too, and as my house became orderly, I felt more "in order" on the inside. Our home group became God's hands and feet and heart in so many ways, reminding us we were not alone. In addition to house cleaning, they provided practical help, like rides to soccer practice for our boys, gifts of money for medical expenses, meals, and, of course, constant prayer.

Interestingly, the love we received in practical acts of service from these kind folks reminded me of someone I'd arranged meals for a few years back. To my shame, I was not as generous of heart as our home group was to us. I organized meals for a mother who had just had another baby, and at some point, I heard she had the audacity to go to her other child's soccer game at the same time she was receiving meals. *Well, that'll never do,* I thought to myself. *If she can go to a soccer game, she can fix a meal for her family.* I cringe remembering that as I write it down.

How like God, who has an uncanny ability to bring full-circle our error onto our own heads, and to put His finger on my sin at just the right time. Now *I* was the one feeling what it was like to barely function. I needed help with mundane things like dinners so that I could do things like go to my kid's soccer games. Mercifully, my home group was more gracious than I had been. Back then, I was so convinced of the righteousness of my own position; unwilling to admit I was wrong. I wish I could confirm to you that I called that mother and apologized. I *think* I did. If she is reading this and I didn't, here it is in black and white: I missed the whole point of helping. I am sorry.

Our home group, thankfully, remained faithful to us for weeks that turned into months. When Bill's ability to cognitively keep up in conversation declined, leading our home group became impossible. So, he asked a young husband and father, Bob, to take over that role. Bob and his wife, Mary, joined our group about a year or so before. When they first came, Bob hammered Bill with questions about the Bible and God and anything else that came into his mind, and soon came to believe in Jesus as his Lord and Savior, as did Mary. They both grew in their biblical understanding at an astronomic rate. As teachers and parents of young twin girls, Bob and Mary were a perfect fit to lead our home bible study. Fortunately, Bob was ready and willing to lead our group, while we continued to host it in our home. Hosting allowed us to enjoy the ongoing community of love and support from everyone in the group, which was a comfort to us at a time when we felt shunned by the leadership of the church.

During this time, I spent hours reading the Bible trying to see if and how our situation mirrored similar stories in the Old and New Testaments. I wanted God to give me some perspective on our predicament, some guidance, some hope, some idea of where He was going with our lives. In addition to the verse in Jeremiah that I read in October 1998 about healing, I wanted to know what other ways He healed people. *Why did God heal? How did He heal? How did He work in the past, so that I might have a clue as to how He would work now?* Then one day, I read the prophecy in 1 Kings 13:2, about a king who would be born and turn the hearts of Israel back to God. His name was Josiah, which means, God heals.

A thought crossed my mind that if God would heal Bill, we could have another baby and name him Josiah, as a living testimony to God's power to heal. It would be a bargain, much like Hannah made when she promised God that if He gave her a son, she'd give him back to God for the rest of his days. God answered Hannah and gave her a son who she named Samuel, and he served in the temple for his whole life.[9] *Hmm...Hannah made a vow to God, and I could too,* I thought. Believing God still works miraculously, as He did in the Bible, I guess you could say I was challenging Him to show me. The reality though, was that I felt somehow *motivated* to ask, as if God was urging me to simply ask. I wrote this vow down in my journal and tucked these thoughts into the back of my mind, making a mental note to talk Bill about it later.

Back then, a couple of the young women from our church and I occasionally met together for play dates with our kids. One morning as the kids played outside and we moms chatted over coffee, I decided to share my harebrained idea with them. "I've decided if God heals Bill, we'll try to have another kid," I announced. "You know, like when Hannah made her bargain with God to have her son Samuel."

---

9   1 Samuel 1:1

They lowered their coffee mugs, raised their eyebrows, and looked at each other, then back to me. I'm not sure which they thought would be the greater miracle, God healing Bill or me having a kid over the age of 40. Never mind the politically incorrect number of kids we already had. These young mothers truly loved us and our kids, and I'm sure they *wanted* to believe God could heal Bill. But the baby idea? Had I lost my mind?

Maybe they thought I was going Kubler-Ross on them: bargaining or denial or some other grieving stage. Often people bargain with God as a common last-ditch effort to save their loved one's life. Even atheists turn to God when the health of someone they love is at stake. Who else but God are you going to call when the doctors have no answers? My thought, though, was that if Hannah could bargain with God and get the baby she asked for, so could I. Worst case scenario, God would say no. And at that point, I simply wasn't above begging. I had nothing to lose.

After I came home from our play date, I thought it was only fair to float my plan with Bill.

"So, Bill, I have this idea."

"Huh?"

"You know how Hannah in the Bible bargained with God to have a son, right? And if God gave her a son, she promised to give him back to the Lord."

"Yeah."

"Well, I made a promise to God. I told Him if He would heal you, we would have another baby if we can."

He looked at me quizzically, then probably remembered, *Yeah, it's Jean I'm talking to.*

"So, what do you think?"

Of course, Bill thought it was a fine idea, no doubt because he thought the chances of it happening were between zero and none. In the past, every time I had a random thought to have another baby, Bill was always right there with me, both literally and figuratively. So, this wasn't entirely out of the ordinary for us. Having a life-threatening illness didn't erase our old patterns of decision-making. *If Jean wants a baby after I'm healed, then that's what we'll do,* Bill probably thought. Maybe it was more like he *hoped* God would heal him. Thankfully, our mustard seed faith is not a hurdle for God to do His work.

Chapter 8:

FACING DISABILITY

We were learning in a deeper way, in this life crisis we found ourselves in, that "God is our Source of life, our Sustainer of life, and the Focus of life."[10] As Bill's identity of "determined guardian" was completely dismantled, the only thing we could do was trust God to provide. Foolish for us to think that He hadn't been doing that all along, whether through Bill, the church or manna from the sky. We'd always given mental assent that God is our Provider throughout our lives, yet when Bill's ability to earn a living was removed, dependence upon God was no longer a theoretical concept. It was real.

One thing I asked God to provide us with was a one-level house for Bill, as his ability to navigate the stairs of our split-level house declined. Finding a single-story house became my obsession, yet my hours spent poring over real estate ads for ramblers produced nothing. A one-level house for a family of eight in our price range was non-existent in our inflated real

---

10   *The Making of a Leader,* by Dr. J. Robert Clinton, page 246.

estate market, so we decided to stay put. God guides us as much through withholding provision as well as giving it, so I hoped this was one of those times. Every time I saw Bill struggling to climb the stairs, though, I wondered if staying in our house was the right thing to do. *Where was the road map for the newly disabled? Were we making the right decision?* So often I felt like we were wandering around in the dark.

Then there was the medical equipment. Did Bill want medical equipment? Of course not. Medical equipment isn't something you add to your birthday or Christmas list, like a flat-screen TV, or a new bike. Bill didn't want medical equipment, and frankly, I didn't want it cluttering up the house. We delayed the acquisition of medical equipment for as long as possible, because, you know, medical equipment is for sick people, or people with disabilities, not Bill. When your identity has been firmly entrenched in being independent, medical equipment is like the Ghost of Christmas Future pointing out that your identity as healthy person is over. This was true for Bill, and by association, for me. He was the disabled now; I was the caregiver. We both held these new identities at arm's length for as long as possible. That is, until a woman whose husband had died of ALS six months before offered us all her husband's medical equipment. I grudgingly acknowledged this could be God's provision, so I invited her over. She and all her medical equipment.

A few nights later, she drove to our house after work with her young son and backed her pickup into the driveway. We unloaded a portable toilet, shower, wheelchair, and a pop-up recliner, and discreetly arranged them in a corner of the garage. It occurred to me that maybe I should cover all the stuff up with a tarp so Bill wouldn't see it, but I didn't have one handy. The dear woman no doubt had conflicting feelings herself; probably happy to get all that stuff out of her house, yet sad to be separating from her late husband's belongings. After we arranged everything, she and her son got back into her truck and drove away. When I turned around, Bill stood in the doorway to the garage leaning on his cane, blinking back tears as he stared at the mountain of medical equipment. Then he turned silently and hobbled back into the house.

The losses continued to pile up. A couple of weeks later, Bill went to the Social Security office to apply for long term disability. He was approved immediately, which was a surprise until he saw his file was marked *Terminal.* Now with all the medical equipment, Social Security disability, and a disabled parking permit, Bill had all the accoutrements of someone he did not want to be, disabled and unable to work. These were for other people, not him.

It was as if God were dragging Bill kicking and screaming into a new world, one where weakness and dependence were character strengths. Wasn't that what the Apostle Paul said? When I am weak, then I am strong? Bill's identity was moving away from what he could *do* to who he *was,* a Christian first, with disabilities or not.

I often felt I was watching these events as if they were scenes of a movie unfolding in front of my eyes. In many ways, I saw them as affecting Bill more than me, which was true. The thought in the back of my mind, though, was that God was writing a story, and the end of it might not be what we were expecting.

Chapter 9:

RESIGNATION

The leadership of our church asked Bill to stand before the congregation in March to formally announce his resignation. Bill didn't want to quit the ministry; he wanted to continue serving in any way he could. However, his offers to serve in a scaled-back or behind-the-scenes role were declined. To their credit, the church continued to provide for half of his salary through benevolence even after his resignation to make up the difference long-term disability didn't pay. For that we were grateful, but we knew benevolence couldn't go on indefinitely. And we were both burdened for our future provision, especially with our large family. It's a common, yet hard lesson in sickness and disability, acknowledging our utter dependence on God. We might think we are our own providers and that the food on the table and the paid mortgage is from our own efforts, yet we were learning again that this isn't the case. Bill was dethroned from the place of provider and saw in real time how God took care of us without any help from him. It was painful, scary, and stretched our faith to a thread.

The past three years had been a steady descent into less physical, and now cognitive, function for Bill. Stepping down from ministry was just the period at the end of a very long sentence. Bill's resignation was a significant loss to both of us. For a man to lose the ability to work to support his family can be tantamount to castration. Bill's identity of "determined guardian" was crushed. And for me, his resignation signaled the end of six years of being a pastor's wife in the middle of a growing ministry to hundreds of people. We entered another dark doorway into increased isolation.

His resignation deflated both of us and depression blanketed us like a fog. Bill went home that day, sat in his recliner, and stared out the window for hours. Everything seemed so final, the sense of rejection, suffocating. It wasn't just that Bill was physically ill with a life-threatening disease. It felt like the leadership of the church no longer had any use for us. We both felt hopeless and unwanted.

Yet, just as a father has compassion on his children, God had compassion on us, and sent a message of hope in the mail the next day. An elderly woman in our church wrote us a letter describing how her mother had been miraculously healed from colon cancer in 1937.

"We really don't know a lot about healing—why some people get healed, and others do not. But we do know God does heal even today. My word for you, Bill and Jean—don't give up. We're praying for you. I know your prayer is that the Lord will be glorified. All my love in Christ, Joan."

I didn't know Joan, but she had attended a class Bill had taught a year or so before. Her boldness in writing to us touched me; I'm sure she had no idea how refreshing her letter was in our lonely desert. *Don't give up*, she said. I read and reread her encouraging words dozens of times, looking for the right words to pray, the right attitude to have, the key to unlock God's treasures of *yes* answers for healing. I didn't find any of that but decided to just keep asking. Joan's letter felt like a message from God that He still miraculously heals, and my job was to simply ask.

Yet even as we prayed for healing, we continued to adapt to the reality of Bill's progressive decline and resignation. And along with our own daily struggles, we became aware of more struggles within our church. A new theological direction with a focus on demons was adopted. Special teams were formed where some would pray for people, while others would prophesy "words" about those people. We disagreed with the new direction, as did many faithful members of the church, who trickled out the back door along with their giving dollars.

Bill officially resigned in March, yet the leadership continued to call him into meetings through the early summer to discuss the financial concerns of the church. The meetings were very confrontational: them accusing Bill of mishandling funds and Bill defending himself. It was odd because the previous December our church had passed an outside audit reporting that the finances were fine. Bill was confused by their anger and felt unjustly attacked. Then in June he was called in to a meeting where the root of the suspicions we had been sensing came to light. Someone—who was anonymous to Bill—apparently had a "word" that Bill had a demon, which allegedly not only had caused his illness but was also on mission to bring down the church. Now all the suspicion and shunning started to make sense.

In the Bible, the Pharisees also accused Jesus of having a demon[11] so I figured we must be in good company. However, in my mind it was past time for Bill to quit going to these meetings. Nevertheless, Bill agreed to meet one more time with them to have the demon—if there was one—removed. He felt he had nothing to hide and wanted to somehow convince them that he wasn't the enemy.

After Bill left to go to the meeting, I knelt beside our bed begging God for answers. The old rose print of our comforter was soaked with my tears as I cried for God to tell me, *what have we done? Why do they seem to hate us?*

---

11   John 8:48-49.

Will this ever be over? Dear Lord, will they ever believe Bill that he honestly loves this church? God, please vindicate him.

A few hours later, Bill came home, climbed up the stairs with his cane and slumped into one of the wingback chairs in the living room.

I sat down beside him. "How did it go?"

"Not good."

"Did they find a demon?"

"Apparently not."

"Well then, that's good, right?"

"No. They think that either there isn't a demon, or that it's bigger than any other they've ever dealt with."

"You're kidding."

"No."

Bill and I believe demons can cause illness as they did to the Old Testament prophet, Job, as well as in the New Testament with the Apostle Paul. Yet in neither account is the conclusion drawn that Job or Paul were somehow responsible for their sickness, even if it *was* caused by demons. In fact, when Job's friends accused him of bringing about his illness because of sin, God called these so-called friends to account.[12] In our case, what was discouraging wasn't the suggestion that demons could be at the root of Bill's illness, it was the suspicion, blaming and shunning that was so painful.

The next day Bill had a regularly scheduled appointment with his doctor. After the usual neurological exam, Dr. Stewart unexpectedly launched into a story about overzealous church leaders. He described how years before when he was a young resident doctor in California, he knew of a man whose church accused him of having a demon. Evidently the man hadn't taken his medicine and subsequently displayed symptoms of mental illness that his

---

12   Job 42:7-8.

church diagnosed as being demonic in origin. Dr. Stewart intervened with
the church leadership on the man's behalf, and the situation was peace-
fully resolved.

Bill and I were stunned. Dr. Stewart told us this story *before* we mentioned anything about what he had just gone through with our church. We
briefly described what was going on, and his counsel was that quite often
when people are convinced of something, they won't change their minds,
even when presented with evidence against their position. Before we left his
office, he shared a few other instances where Christians accused each other
of having demons, and the resultant wreckage left behind. Our time with
Dr. Stewart seemed like a divine appointment and gave us a comforting and
objective view of our situation.

One might ask why we didn't leave the church right then. I believe it
was a lack of faith, and fear, plain and simple. For all the conflict we were
experiencing, the church was providing half of Bill's income through benevolence. It was a lack of faith on our part and so we stayed.

The following month, Bill met with one of the leaders and explained
how their actions had hurt us, and as suddenly as it all began, the leadership
apologized for the whole thing. I was beyond relieved that their suspicion
seemed to be over, and asked God to help me forgive. *Lord, restore to Bill and
I our joy. Please lift me out of this depression. And thank You so much this is over.*

Unfortunately, we found out later that it really wasn't over. Our theological beliefs over how much power demons have over Christians diverged
too much with theirs to allow true unity between us and the leadership. Yet
as believers in Jesus Christ, we should be able to agree to disagree on matters
that are open-handed issues. Because we don't always know what we think
we know, especially when it comes to the things unseen.

In hindsight, maybe there was a temptation to come up with a reason
as to why Bill was sick. That was the conclusion Job's friends came to in the
Old Testament book of Job. If Job would simply repent, then all his misery

would go away. And in fact, Satan *did* cause Job's miseries. But his friends were in error to *blame* Job. The reality is suffering is a common theme in the Bible. And just as suffering is a common theme in the Bible, so is betrayal. In his book, *Walking with God through Pain and Suffering*, Tim Keller describes how in the Old Testament Joseph was betrayed by his brothers yet was able to see God's hand behind even the hard circumstances of his life. This enabled him to forgive his brothers for selling him into slavery. "This biblical realism, to see clearly the two aspects of every event—on the one hand, human mishandling (and the blind work of nature), and on the other the perfect will of God…was to be supremely exemplified in Gethsemane, where Jesus accepted his betrayal as "the cup which the Father has given me. "[13]

Likewise, God helped us see this reality in the two aspects of our situation: Bill's illness and the conflict in our church. The Lord used this conflict to teach us to look to Him for meaning in our trials. Rather than focus only on our perceived injustices and hurt, we tried to focus on what God was teaching us. Psalm 66:10-12 was a comfort to us during this season: "For You, O God, have tested us; You have refined us as silver is refined. You brought us into the net; You laid affliction on our backs. You have caused men to ride over our heads; We went through fire and through water; But You brought us out to rich *fulfillment*."

---

13   *Walking with God Through Pain and Suffering,* by Tim Keller. Note 363. Kidner, Genesis, p. 207.

Chapter 10:

HELP

Often there isn't a clear line of demarcation between healthy and sick. Illness often progresses slowly and insidiously until much of what 'used to be' is no more. This was the case for Bill. His symptoms developed over time and ebbed and flowed with no particular pattern. His good days were gradually eclipsed by bad days. As his ability to take care of himself declined, I'd like to say that my care of him seamlessly increased. However, it didn't. In my sometimes-misguided attempts to maintain Bill's sense of autonomy, I was usually three steps behind when my caregiving should ratchet up.

One morning I left Bill alone at home for a while so I could do some yard work at a ministry house close to the local college. The house was a 100-year-old structure with weeds dating back to at least 1963. Fortunately, pulling weeds meshed with my need to work out my caregiving anxieties. Gardening was a convenient stress outlet and cheaper than Xanax. After the kids went to school, and I made sure Bill was situated at home, I kissed him goodbye and drove two miles away to the weed pile in front of the old house.

After a couple of hours digging in the dirt, I got a frantic call from the nurse at our doctor's office. "Mrs. Sullivan, we have Bill here at the office. He isn't doing very well—you better get down here right away."

She sounded rather stressed, almost to the point of needing to pull weeds. I threw my garden tools in the van and may have broken a few laws on my way down the freeway. Fingers gripping the wheel, I kept repeating, *"Lord, please help Bill. Please help him to be okay."* I did a power slide into the parking lot at the doctor's office and ran into the waiting room, where the receptionist quickly ushered me into the hallway leading to the exam rooms. I found Bill sitting alone in one of the rooms, bearing a remarkable resemblance to Christopher Lloyd's character, Emmett "Doc" Brown, in the movie *Back to The Future*.

Apparently after I left him that morning, Bill became anxious and began to pace up and down our hallway at home. I don't know why he didn't call me—*or did he and I didn't answer?* He told me later how disoriented he became, and how it seemed he was watching himself from the ceiling, hearing himself yelling and thinking he shouldn't be screaming, but just couldn't stop. Somehow, he got himself together enough to drive the three miles to the doctor's office, get out of his truck, and address the doctor's receptionists with an outside voice while complaining about the large Methodist spiders on the walls. They hustled him back to a private exam room and pieced together that we had forgotten to change his pain patch on time, which should have happened the day before. He was going into withdrawals.

Oh. Note to self: *We have officially crossed the state line and are no longer in Kansas. Bill is not autonomous—he needs my constant attention. Change pain patch every three days instead of relying on Bill to remember!!*

As Bill required more one-on-one attention, and I got a clue, my focus and energy zeroed in on his needs. Projects that didn't need to get done didn't get done. My weeding days—at the ministry house and my house—were over and my garden showed it. The unkempt planting beds I saw from our second floor living room window were a daily reminder that I had neither the time nor the energy to do anything about them.

I never considered myself a person who had difficulty accepting help from anyone. For some people, root canals are preferable to accepting help from others. Not me. My problem was that when people said, "Just call me if you need anything," I didn't know what to tell them. What did they mean by *anything?* Did they mean cooking a meal? Babysitting? Mowing the yard? What if I asked them to clean my filthy toilet and they were thinking more along the lines of picking up the mail? I didn't want to ask the wrong thing, so most of the time when people said, "Call me if you need anything," I simply didn't.

Even if people asked me what I needed, I was so overwhelmed with Bill, the kids, and remembering to breathe in and out, I couldn't give them a straight answer. If you've never lived through a crisis or long-term caregiving, you may not realize that sometimes caregivers need someone to tell *them* what they need. My finite number of brain cells were occupied with dosing schedules, doctor's appointments, and calculating how old the kids were going to be when their dad died. That's it. If I had to answer the question, "What do you need?" I would've said, "You know what? I need someone to do everything except shave my legs."

There were people, though, who didn't wait for me to call them. They just barged in. Barging in is usually frowned upon in our *I'm fine, everything's fine, and no, my eye isn't twitching* culture. No one wants to intrude into anyone's 'personal business.' But if I'm drowning, I *want* someone to notice the water lapping up under my chin and intrude already! I don't want them scratching their heads wondering if I'll take offense if they save my life. Save me first and then we can discuss the finer details of how they threw the rope. People who take it upon themselves to see and act without written instructions are gifts from God. We need to be those people to others, too.

Kim is a person who barges in. She worked at a trauma hospital where jumping in and saving lives is what they're trained and paid to do. Kim cared for burn victims, distracting them while their wounds were being cleaned and rewrapped. She knew a thing or two about how to help stressed-out people in crisis.

She called me one day and announced, "Our home group is coming to clean up your yard." As I looked out the window at the knee-high weeds in my yard, I pretended to protest. "Oh, you don't have to do that—"

"Forget it. This is good for us. We need to do this for you guys."

A few days later a convoy of trucks drove into our cul-de-sac and parked in front of our house. Kim's landscaping crew got out hauling wheelbarrows, lawnmowers, edgers—the works. About ten people descended on our yard to edge, weed the overgrown flower beds, and mow the knee-high grass. The crew's finishing touch was rich, dark mulch that brilliantly contrasted with the flats of cheerful yellow, orange, and purple flowers. As soon as their work was done, they packed up and left, their mission accomplished.

Happiness, joy, and rapture filled my heart as I looked out onto my yard that summer. When everything outside was neat and organized, I felt neat and organized. My mind relaxed. Once again, God reminded me that He loved us and was walking through this valley with us.

Our own home group also didn't wait for us to tell them what we needed. Along with the house cleaning they arranged for us, one of the couples left a card on the coffee table before they left one night. After they left, Bill and I opened it up and read:

Dear Bill & Jean,

While praying for healing one night, we felt led to help with the financial needs that can go along with an illness. Please accept this in that regard.

For His glory.

It was a check for $1500. Generous. Unrequested. And another tangible evidence of God's care for us through His church.

Being around other caregivers who live the disability dream also helped me persevere through this time. There's a deep connection when you walk into another one's dark places with them. C.S. Lewis put it aptly: "Friendship is born at that moment when one man says to another: 'What! You too? I thought that no one but myself.'" Mardee was that person for me. Her husband struggles with a different neuromuscular disease but one with similar symptoms as Bill. Before our husbands got sick, Mardee and I launched a ministry that provided practical help and meals for people in need. Ironically, we now found ourselves on the receiving end of that help. We often met for coffee to commiserate about the emotional and physical toll of caring for our husbands.

Proverbs 25:11 states that "a word fitly spoken is like apples of gold in settings of silver." For me, words written in cards and letters that came in the little box at the end of our street were those apples of gold. Snail mail letters in our mailbox with stamps and stuff. My friend Kathy's letters were those apples of gold. Years later, they still are! Kathy, a schoolteacher, laced her letters with stories about her classroom or her own kids' shenanigans. Written on stationery, cards, or simple white printer paper she'd scavenged somewhere, every note included newsy anecdotes about her husband's organic farm, like how covering tomatoes plants with red plastic makes the tomatoes jealous so they grow stronger. She always ended each letter reassuring me of their prayers for us. God must've whispered in her ear to send them so they arrived on the exact days I needed most to know someone cared. Those letters were God's love in an envelope to me.

Chapter 11:

PROVISION

Bill's biggest emotional burden in all of this was the thought of leaving me with six kids with no means of support. Fortunately, we had secured a bit of life insurance before Bill got sick, which gave me a couple of years to go to college and earn whatever degree that was most-likely-to-feed-and-house-six-kids. Bill and I even got life insurance for our kids—just in case. Beyond that, his goal was to do everything in his power to leave us "situated." Routine conversations often went like this:

"I don't want you to have to worry about house repairs."

"Like when you're dead?"

"Yeah."

"Okay."

We decided to refinance the house like everyone did back in the day, and got new carpeting installed. Then our brothers-in-law and friends came and demoed the rotted kitchen cabinets, countertops and janky appliances and replaced them all. The last thing that went in was a laminate kitchen floor. Loads of backbreaking fun.

A few mornings later, I got up to fix a pot of coffee and sloshed into the kitchen. The floor was soaking wet, and the floating laminate floor was literally *floating*. After some investigation, Bill discovered that the PVC tube connecting the icemaker in the refrigerator had ruptured. When he looked closer at the plastic tubing, it appeared to have tiny bite marks on it. We concluded that a mouse must have used it to floss.

We called our homeowner's insurance company. "Yeah, it looks like a mouse chewed through it."

"Are you *sure* a mouse chewed through it? Are you *sure* it didn't just spontaneously rupture?"

"Nope—looks like a mouse."

"Well, if it spontaneously ruptured we'd cover that, but if it's damage caused by vermin we don't," the insurance rep said.

"Oh."

Apparently when the new housing development went up in the next block, all the little field mice moved into our neighborhood—some into our house—and ruined our ice maker tubing and new floor. The floor installer estimated the cost to replace it would be around $1,000.

The next morning, on April 12, 2000, I wrote in my journal: *One request: our floor was ruined in the kitchen when mice chewed through the water line from the faucet to the refrigerator. Water got under the wood floor and buckled it up. Please, Lord, provide for us there.*

God did not delay His provision. It seemed that for every need we had, He had an answer. Later *that day*, a check from a friend came in the mail for $1,000. Our friend did not know about our floor disaster. It was a 'coincidence' that they sent a check for the exact amount we needed. We experienced again that God's faithfulness really is new every morning.[14]

As grateful as we were for God's provision for our physical needs, we needed His help for our emotional needs too. Like little birds constantly squawking for *more, more,* we craved God's moment-by-moment presence. I needed to *know* He was with us all the time. The moment I forgot that, or somehow didn't feel it, I'd slip into depression. My pendulum swung from gratitude for something God had done, to pleading for Him to explain why all this was happening in the first place.

"Please forgive me for my depression and sadness over what has happened to Bill and his job," I wrote in April. "He seems so sad over what he has lost, and I feel anger that things happened the way they did. Please give us renewed hope, renewed purpose, renewed joy, and anticipation. Please comfort Bill and heal him completely."

A few days later God brought to mind a verse from Romans 8:27, "Now He who searches the hearts knows what the mind of the Spirit *is,* because He makes intercession for the saints according to *the will* of God." It was as if He were saying to me, "My Spirit is praying for you, so you need to quit worrying." *Quit worrying—right,* I thought. Easy to say, harder to do. I didn't know where Bill's illness was going, how long, or how bad it would be. There was no roadmap. And that thing about walking by faith, not by sight? I didn't like that either.

God was patient with me and again comforted Bill with renewed hope, purpose, and joy. He broke into Bill's awareness in a special way one Sunday morning while I was at church and he was at home because he wasn't feeling well. I walked in the door after the service and asked him how his morning went.

---

14   Lamentations 3:23.

"I was praying while you guys were at church," he said, "and I had this weird sense of God's peace just washing over me."

"Oh?"

"Yes, and I was thinking of how great it'll be to be in heaven where there's no pain, no sin—just Jesus."

Wow...I hoped he wasn't being prophetic, as in this 'going to heaven' business was imminent. Dismissing that idea, I thanked God for comforting Bill and whispered a promise that I would try to keep trusting Him. Trusting, of course, did not preclude questions. Sometimes I felt like a 4-year-old asking *Why? What sin are we not aware of which has caused this all to happen to us? Why have you allowed this?* Jesus' disciples asked questions, so I figured questions were allowed.

There is a story in the book of John where the disciples ask Jesus to explain why a man was blind. Was it his parents' sin or his? Jesus' reply in John 9:3 was "Neither this man nor his parents sinned, but that the works of God should be revealed in him." I wondered if that was the case for us. Was God wanting to do something through us, or in us, that I was simply unaware of? I continued reading a few chapters further where Jesus said in John 16:24, "Until now you have asked nothing in My name. Ask, and you will receive, that your joy may be full."

I would love for my joy to be full, I thought. *But was asking for Bill to be healed too much?* I eventually figured that God could decide if it was too much or not and simply continued to beg for Bill to be healed.

Chapter 12:

PSP SYMPOSIUM

At the end of April, I flew to Los Angeles to attend a symposium on Progressive Supranuclear Palsy at UCLA. My sister, Rebecca, was in LA that weekend too. We made plans to meet for an early dinner after the conference was over at 3 p.m.

Before I left the hotel in Westwood that morning, I sat down to write in my journal. A random thought occurred to me that although I'd taught a spiritual gifts class, I didn't know much about prophetic gifts. My Christian experience was quite conservative as opposed to charismatic, but I wrote in my journal a request that God would send someone to tell me about prophecy. I didn't know why I wrote that, but for some reason I thought maybe God had something to say on the matter.

I closed my journal, put my room key and black portfolio into my bag, and walked a few blocks to the PSP symposium. I entered the dark auditorium where the speakers and panelists were seated up front, and lots of people and families affected by PSP in one way or another filled in the rows. In one of the breakout sessions I noticed that everyone on the panel was over 50 years old, and most were over 60. Bill's diagnosis at the age of 40 was rare, to say the least. As I listened to the panelists describe their experiences with PSP, one woman shared how the disease had robbed her of the plans she and her husband had for their retirement. *Retirement?* I thought to myself. I *wished* Bill was going to live to retirement age. My mind drifted to our six kids back home growing up without their dad, and I could barely contain my bitterness.

Although the organizers tried to put a positive spin on the event, all I came away with was how crappy the disease was, and how Bill was way too young to have it. There weren't many options to help with his symptoms, and there definitely weren't any cures. All they could offer were tips on how to care for someone with PSP. It's called *palliative care.* The last thing they requested was for each caregiver to *please consider filling out this form to donate your loved one's brain to research.* After the conference was over, I grabbed my portfolio, stuffed it into my bag and walked out into the California sunshine.

Rebecca was waiting outside, and we walked a couple of blocks over to a Mexican restaurant in Westwood Village, an upscale neighborhood with streets lined with clipped hedges, birds of paradise shrubs, palm trees, and posh boutiques. Warm and sunny, almost like a Disneyland for adults. It was a welcome change from our soggy Pacific Northwest and my 24/7 caregiving duties.

The hostess showed us a booth, the server brought us chips, salsa and two glasses of wine, and we caught up on each other's lives.

Rebecca asked, "So how did it go?"

"Okay, I guess. I learned everything I didn't want to know about balance problems and retirement. How are you guys?"

"I have the coolest story to tell you." I picked up a chip and asked, "What's that?"

"I've been feeling out of sorts spiritually."

"Oh?"

"Yeah, I'm doing all this study about Christian leadership, but I've been feeling a little spiritually anemic. Learning a new job, looking for a new house, and flying back and forth from Oklahoma City to LA every weekend to take classes at Biola. I haven't been spending much time with God, and I've been feeling guilty about it."

"I'm sorry…"

"No, this is cool. Larry and I visited a new church last weekend, Easter Sunday, and the pastor stood up at the end of the service and asked if anyone had any words for anyone."

"What do you mean, *words*?"

Rebecca's and my experience growing up in church did not include prophetic "words." Prophetic words happened in churches where people swung on chandeliers. And, of course, there was the word that Bill had a demon, so that didn't conjure up warm thoughts. However, I recalled my journal entry that morning, asking God to speak to me regarding prophetic gifts, as what 1 Corinthians 14:3 describes: "But he who prophesies speaks edification and exhortation and comfort to men."

Rebecca continued, "So, a woman stood up at the end of the service and motioned to us. Jean, I've never seen this lady before in my life. I didn't know who she was. But she stood up, motioned to us and we stood up too. Then she said to us, 'God loves you, He knows you love Him, and He's with you in this move.'"

"You're kidding."

"Nope."

"Rebecca, I just wrote about word gifts in my journal this morning, and I asked God to send someone to me to speak something to me," I said.

I wasn't quite sure why the subject of prophetic words came up that day. Maybe God wanted to remind us not to be cynical or unbelieving when people encourage us with messages only He can send. As 1 Thessalonians

5:20-21 says, "Do not despise prophecies. Test all things; hold fast what is good." Maybe God was reminding us that the Christian life *should* be supernatural, not boringly predictable as it might seem sometimes. Isn't that what we sign up for when we follow Jesus—a living relationship with the God of the universe who knows everything, can do anything, and loved us enough to die for our sins?

The next day was Sunday and we decided to throw caution to the wind and visit a church that makes no apologies for its charismatic leanings. During the service, there was a time to share prayer requests with those sitting around us. A woman named Margaret was sitting next to me, and she reached out, touched my arm, and asked me if I had anything she could pray for me about. Why is it that the most benign acts of kindness trigger our deepest emotions? The compassion behind her question opened the floodgates of my eyes and heart. "My husband…" I felt the tears begin to sting my eyes, "I want God to heal him." I barely got the words out before dissolving into embarrassed sobs. She immediately bowed her head and asked God to heal Bill, simply and without a lot of fanfare. Almost like she believed He could do it.

Chapter 13:

PRAYERS

didn't share with many people the vow I had made to God, that if He would heal Bill, we'd have another child. I didn't share with many people the verse about healing in Jeremiah 30:17 that I felt God had given me in 1998. Yet, a collection of people who were unrelated to one another began praying for Bill to be healed, including a woman who called us one evening in early May.

I have no idea how she got our number…maybe someone at church gave it to her? There was a bit of a language barrier; as a Korean immigrant, English was her second language. What came through loud and clear, though, was that she'd been praying for Bill's healing, and believed he was going to be healed very soon. In fact, when she called, she asked if he was healed yet! We had never met this woman, didn't know her at all. In fact, I can't tell you who she is today.

While Bill was talking on the phone with her, I went upstairs into the living room and looked out our picture window. A woman named Patty was parked in front of our house. I didn't know Patty very well, except that she attended a class Bill had taught at church. I also didn't know why she came over every day, parked her truck in front of our house, and prayed for Bill. Patty would sit there in her truck for about half an hour, then get out and put a sticky note with a verse on our door and leave. It creeped me out, to tell you the truth. Kind of like if a few shepherds showed up when your first kid was born. Even so, what a comfort to me she was, apparently obeying a divine directive to intercede for us. All I could figure was God put her up to it, and she had the audacious faith to obey.

Another friend stopped me outside the church kitchen after a service one Sunday night. "Jean, I keep praying for Bill to be healed," her eyes glistening, "but don't know if healing is my will or God's." That was the question of the hour. I didn't have the answer. I also wanted Bill to be healed, but I didn't know if God *wanted* that. I struggled with the idea that if this wasn't God's idea, then maybe my prayers were pointless. I would think that and then sure enough, someone else would tell me they were praying for Bill to be healed, too.

Yet another friend, Tammy, pulled me aside in a quiet hallway at our church, looked over my shoulder and whispered, "God wakes me up in the middle of the night to pray for Bill to be healed." After losing her newborn son years before, Tammy was well acquainted with grief. She and her husband knew from bitter experience that God doesn't always heal. But something, or *Someone,* was prompting her to pray for Bill. Even another friend's 10-year-old daughter prayed for Bill to be healed every night when she was getting tucked into bed.

Granted, when a well-loved, well-known person in a small community gets sick, people pray. Nowadays, social media sites are flooded with stories of people struggling with life-threatening conditions, with calls to pray for healing. Back in 2000, however, there was no Facebook. Besides, who in their right mind would ask for complete healing for someone who had a type of Parkinson's? Parkinson's, or in Bill's case—PSP—is something you manage. Quality of life and symptom control are the goals. Complete and total healing are not expected.

But people kept insisting they were praying for Bill's *complete* healing. Who else could have been orchestrating this but God? Yet, as I watched this unfold, I didn't want to assume that what I wanted was what God was going to do. I even questioned whether to involve my kids in praying specifically for their dad's healing. What would happen to their faith if Bill died—would they hate God for denying their request? Would they become bitter against Him? What if God didn't heal and they wondered if He existed *at all?* On the other hand, what if they did pray for their dad to be healed and God healed him? After going back and forth in my mind countless times, I finally decided it wasn't my responsibility to control the outcome but to just to ask. It was God's job to decide what the answer was. So, every day the kids prayed for their dad to be healed. And every day we waited.

Now this didn't mean that we hid the truth of his condition from them. We didn't. Without overwhelming them with the sordid details, we gave them all the updates from the doctors. And they saw with their own eyes when Bill grimaced and hobbled with his cane to our bedroom to lie down. They saw him drinking instant breakfast because he couldn't swallow food. They heard his slurred words; they saw him choke on food at the dinner table.

Our older children were stoic in their outward display of emotion. If they had any anxiety, it usually manifested as misbehavior or anger. Only rarely would I get a glimpse of fear their father might die. Our oldest son, Taylor, was a teen then, and recounted a time he was driving his dad somewhere when Bill suddenly got car sick from the motion of the truck. Bill wore a motion sickness patch behind his ear, but sometimes it just wasn't enough to keep the dizziness and nausea at bay. They were headed down a busy four lane highway without shoulders on either side, and nowhere to stop. So, Bill motioned to Taylor to keep going while he emptied his stomach contents out the window.

The bottom line was the kids knew their dad was very sick. Maybe the seriousness of his condition gave more urgency to their prayers? Maybe more faith? I don't know. But the morning after the Korean woman called us, little Olivia prayed, "I thank you that Daddy is going to be healed soon." Simple, to the point, her childlike faith caught me off guard. How could she say that with such *confidence?*

At the end of May, old friends of ours, Tony and Debbie, came to visit us. Tony and Bill had worked together in Southern California, and then again at an environmental engineering company in Washington. Tony shared how God was leading him, too, to specifically ask for Bill's healing. He told us how he prayed for another friend who was gravely ill and how God brought him back from the brink of death through prayer. "Debbie and I are praying for you to be healed, too," he assured Bill.

Then in August, Bill's brother, Kevin, his wife, Chris, and their kids came up from California to visit our extended family in Washington. Their three children, Courtney, Nick, and Connor were the same ages as 18-year-old Taylor, 12-year-old Andy and 7-year-old Jack—in fact, their son Connor shares a birthday with Jack. Bill looked forward to visiting with Kevin and hoped he'd feel well enough to enjoy their time together.

Kevin is older than Bill by four years and taught Bill how to throw a football, how to drive a stick in a '65 VW, and how to roll a joint—essential life skills for (some!) growing up as baby boomers in Southern California. They tag-teamed each other through life, both marrying young and enduring divorces within a few years of each other and both repenting and coming to faith in Christ as adults.

Kevin and Chris pulled into our driveway, their kids tumbled out of their van, and it took all of about ten minutes for the kids to start chasing each other around our back yard. The youngest children had never met each other but could easily have been mistaken for brothers and sisters—stair-stepped Sullivan's with sun-kissed skin and mischievous eyes. Bill felt pretty well, so we loaded up the van with a picnic dinner and drove to a nearby park. I got lots of pictures of the kids dangling between the railings of the jungle gym, posing at the top of the slide, and flying high on the swings. After a couple of hours visiting around the evergreen shaded picnic table, we packed up and I drove our van back to our house so Bill could rest.

Kevin watched Bill lean back and grimace. Kevin's brows drew together and he asked, "So how are you doing, Bill?"

"I've got some pain ... a little trouble breathing," he said.

"Our whole church has been praying for you ..."

"I appreciate that—tell them thanks."

"I will." Kevin's eyes welled up as he got up and put his hand on his younger brother's shoulder.

Chris knelt on the floor in front of Bill, holding his hands in hers. "You know, we came up here to visit the family," Chris said, "but what we really came here for was to ask God to heal you."

Kevin wiped his eyes and began, "God, we know nothing is impossible for You. Nothing. Jesus, You healed the sick and raised the dead when You were on earth, and we believe You can do that for Bill. Please, Lord ... please heal my brother. Please heal Bill."

One box of Kleenex later, Kevin and Chris gathered up their kids, got in their car and left to return home.

So many people all asking for the same thing: Bill's complete healing. This wasn't normal. This seemed supernatural. I kept these things written in my journal and daily turned them over and over in my mind. It truly seemed that God was up to something big.

Chapter 14:

SUMMER'S END

The end of summer brought a sense of reflection and resignation to my mind regarding our situation. Bill was getting weaker and spent many hours each day in bed. I clucked around after the kids, trying to keep them quiet for their dad, while attempting to put on a calm face of reassurance for them. Throughout this time, I swung between having peace about our situation and sinking into depression. Confident that God was in control, and fear that He wasn't. The burden of keeping a stiff upper lip for the kids was exhausting. In the quiet times alone in my room, reading and praying, depression crept in when I had time to think. When there was no busyness to distract me, the very real possibility of Bill's death loomed over me. I clung to the Scriptures, especially laments from the book of Psalms.

"How long, Lord?

Will You hide Yourself forever?

Will Your wrath burn like fire?

Remember how short my time is;

> For what futility have You created all the children of men?
>
> What man can live and not see death?
>
> Can he deliver his life from the power of the grave?
>
> Lord, where *are* Your former lovingkindnesses,
>
> *Which* You swore to David in Your truth?
>
> Psalm 89:46-49

I just wished God would heal Bill and allow him to return to some job or ministry. I begged God to restore something of what we had lost. I didn't delude myself that God would heal him if He wasn't going to; I knew Bill could die from PSP and felt a responsibility to prepare for it. Like a Slinky toy sliding from one hand to another, one moment I'd brace myself for Bill's death, and the next I'd beg God to heal him. Somehow, I knew God would do what was best for us, but I wanted Him, I dithered God constantly, to bless Bill with health again.

When the new school year was about to begin, I decided to home-school the four youngest: Andy, David, Jack, and Olivia. My thought was that if they were learning at home, they'd spend more time with their father, precious time that was running out. I made all the arrangements with the school district, ordered curriculum and supplies, and signed up for gym classes at the local YMCA.

Taylor graduated from high school the previous June and wanted to go to college, but we had no money to send him, and we weren't inclined to take out student loans. The wages from his job at the ice cream store would just barely cover the cost of books and gas. "I don't want to make an appointment to register for classes if we don't have the money," Taylor told me one morning. I appreciated his practicality, but I thought we might float the idea with God first, and if He provided the money, then maybe Taylor could go to college.

"Well, why don't you go ahead and make the appointment, and we'll ask God if He would provide what you need?" I said.

"Okay," he said, sighing at me before dialing the phone.

A few hours later, Bill's mom called. "Hi Jean, how are you all getting along?" she asked.

"Pretty good. The kids are ready for school to begin, and Bill's doing okay."

"Well, Poppie and I want to know if you guys have any specific financial needs..."

"Uh, I don't know," I said, replaying the conversation with Taylor from that morning in my mind.

"Well, do you think it would be helpful if we paid off your van?" she asked. *Help?* I thought. *Yes, that would help. It would be a huge help!* I was a bit overwhelmed with her offer and didn't know what to say. "Wow. Thank you so much. Thank you," I stammered. They brought a check by the house the next day for the amount we owed on the van, plus $1,000 more. That $1,000 covered Taylor's community college tuition exactly—another evidence God was taking care of every detail of our lives. It helped me to see God in every day, every circumstance, every discouraging time, every happy time. I asked Him to take me outside of my preoccupation with myself and my problems to see Him at work around me.

And as God encouraged us with answers to prayer, I also was constantly aware that He might not answer "yes" to my desire for Bill be healed. *"Help me to accept this time with Bill's illness may get worse and worse and worse—for a long time, and You may not choose to heal him this side of heaven,"* I wrote. *"That is Your decision. I submit to Your will, and Your plan and Your wisdom. Just fill us up to overflowing with Yourself, and an awareness of Your love and power. You are perfect in all Your ways, and they are, indeed, past finding out."* Journal, September 6, 2000.

I continually rehearsed both scenarios in my mind: God healing Bill/
God not healing Bill. I wanted to be prepared for whatever happened, and I
didn't want to assume that just because I prayed constantly for God to heal
Bill that He would do that. But being the control freak I am, I wanted God
to tell me what He was going to do.

Then I remembered from reading stories of healing in the Bible that
people don't have to be convinced in their minds God *will* heal for Him *to*
heal. The old saw that if you just have faith, or if you just believe, somehow
makes God obligated to heal your loved one has zero scriptural basis. I had
faith God *could* heal, but I had no absolute certainty He *would* heal. He hadn't
sent me His calendar, His agenda, His to-do list for the Sullivan's. I didn't
know what He was going to do. But in retrospect, I can see that beginning in
September, there seemed to be some clues. Call me a wacko, but this actually
happened—you can't make this stuff up.

*We got the October Reader's Digest today, and in it was an article about
miracles. Interesting, because I always have had a thought in the back of my mind
about God healing Bill in October. Mostly because God has brought to mind two
significant verses in October, once in October of '98, Jeremiah 30:17, and once
in October of '99, Acts 4:22. Both verses speak of God miraculously healing, both
spiritually and physically. Oddly enough, the new Reader's Digest for the month of
October has an article on miracles. I was also thinking just now, if God does heal
Bill, we will have a testimony people will want to hear. Especially since our story
includes so many spiritual and emotional struggles not to mention the physical
problems. I wonder if it is God's will to heal Bill in October. Sure would be an
interesting conclusion to an arduous journey. I guess I should pray like Daniel
did, when he concluded from reading Jeremiah that the 70 years in Babylon were
almost over: "We do not present our supplications before You because of our
righteous deeds, but because of Your great mercies." Daniel 9:18. Bill and I
don't ask God to heal him because we deserve it, but because we are pleading for
God to be merciful to us. We are at His mercy; we have no other hope.* Journal,
September 14, 2000

As that summer of isolation closed, I felt like a chapter of our lives was closing, too. The ending wasn't clear to me yet, and the scary fact was... things could go either way.

Chapter 15:

ANTICIPATION

ord, help me to know how to pray for Bill, our kids, for the church. Sometimes I have all these thoughts swirling around in my head, and I don't know which of them are from You, and which are from my own nutty ideas. Please heal Bill. Please finish the work in us You wanted to do through this illness, and then heal him. And after You heal him, tell us what to do. Help us to live in a way that pleases You, honors You, and accomplishes all You want to do through us in the power of Your Spirit. Journal, October 9, 2000

I had an unexplainable, almost tangible sense of anticipation throughout the month of October. Toward the end of the month, we were at Bill's parents' home, celebrating their birthdays and wedding anniversary. As we always did before eating a meal there, Bill, his parents, sisters, brothers-in-law and assorted nieces and nephews were standing in a circle in the kitchen, hands held, heads bowed, and together we recited the Lord's Prayer. Just as we got to the line "for Thine is the Kingdom and the power, and the glory forever," I thought, *How cool would it be if RIGHT THEN God would heal Bill?*

But...He didn't.

I looked around and hoped no one could read my silly thoughts and conclude I was delusional and needed a doctor as much as Bill. I was disappointed and wondered if I was asking God for too much or for something He didn't want to do.

As for Bill's doctors, they kept telling us the same thing: the prognosis for Progressive Supranuclear Palsy is grim. People who have it typically die from complications of immobility—usually pneumonia—within five to seven years of diagnosis. Mulling over where Bill's health was at this point, I figured we were on the tail end of that time. He had been using a cane for two years, he choked on food and could only eat soft, thick instant breakfast, he was forgetful, he didn't initiate conversation, and he had a flat expression on his face. He was in constant pain on his whole left side which was also very weak. He had balance problems and would fall backwards if he wasn't intentionally leaning forward when he stood up. In addition to the balance problems, he suffered from vertigo and would often throw up on car rides to the doctor, which was about the only place he ever went anymore. He couldn't direct his eyes and had stopped reading. And, no surprise, he was depressed.

It was in those circumstances we came to the end of October.

Chapter 16:

GOD'S POWER
DISPLAYED

Even though I'd grown up in a church tradition which included events like tent meetings and revivals, most of the revivals I knew about were along the lines of pre-programmed Wednesday night meetings, with the word "REVIVAL" strategically displayed on the reader board in front of the church, so in the event God read it, He'd be sure to put it on His calendar to be there too.

Pseudo-revivals don't negate authentic revivals, however, just like counterfeit money doesn't negate the real thing. The Great Awakening in the 1740's with the preaching of Jonathan Edwards and George Whitfield is an example of a bona fide revival. The Jesus Movement of the late '60s-early '70's is another. My family attended Calvary Chapel in the early 70's, when crowds of hippies came in and sat down on the floor when the pews filled up as Pastor Chuck Smith taught through the Bible. Many turned away from their addictions and followed Jesus in genuine faith.

Our current church was experiencing something too, which resembled more of an exodus than a revival, to be honest. Right in the middle of it, in October of 2000, our church invited a special speaker for a three-night series. Bill went with me the first night but missed the second night because he was too sick. And, yes, the speaker was scheduled to speak about revival, when God comes down in a special way for a season to turn His church from their self-righteous, complacent selves to repentance, as well as change the lives of those who don't know Him yet. Regardless of the conflicted feelings I had toward the leadership of our church, I sensed God was up to something and was fully anticipating that whatever it was might include healing Bill.

On March 13th, I had an impression God would use Bill's healing as a flashpoint for revival. Is today the day? Please come and do Your work, Lord!! And if healing Bill is part of Your plan this week, please answer the prayers of so many faithful saints and do it. Do Your work in us and through us. Journal, October 27, 2000

It was Friday, the last night of the three-night series, and Bill told me he felt well enough to go. Which was great, I thought, because if God was going to heal him, it might be helpful for him to be there. The story when Jesus healed the centurion's servant who wasn't present, but at home at the time, didn't cross my mind, so it could have worked. But whatever the case, I was glad Bill was going.

I told the kids they needed to come, too, and got some pushback from the older ones.

"Why do we have to go to church on a Friday <u>niiiiight</u>?"

"It's important."

"But why? How long is it going to be?"

"Get ready and get in the van in thirty minutes."

Look kids, I thought, *if God heals your dad tonight, you're gonna want to be there and someday you'll thank me.*

We piled into the van and headed to church, which was about a mile away from our house. I pulled into the parking lot, which was already filling up, and helped Bill get out. Inside the church, people milled about before crowding into the rows of seats. We found our usual row and sat down. After a few songs and an opening prayer, the speaker stepped up to the podium and began to teach out of Ephesians 1. He asked, "What limits your life as you follow Christ? Things that are impossible?" He focused on verses 18 - 20, "That you may know ... what is the incomparably great power for us who believe. That power is the same as the mighty strength he exerted when He raised Christ from the dead ..."

He reminded us of the impossibility of someone being raised from the dead, the impossibility of a massive stone at the entrance of a tomb being rolled away. The impossibility of ... my thoughts were interrupted by his next question: "What stone do you need God to roll away in your life?" My eyes stung as I blinked back three years of pleading and begging. *God, I need you to heal Bill.*

When the speaker finished, our pastor stepped up to the microphone and invited people to come up front to pray. I watched as Bill reached for his cane and hobbled to the stage, knelt down on one of the steps and bowed his head. He told me later he felt compelled to go forward and confess his anger toward God for allowing him to get sick.

Surprisingly to me, the elders surrounded Bill and began praying for him, while the pastor also asked the church to pray for him to be healed. Four hundred people got on their knees, their voices filling the room as they prayed for God to heal Bill. Friends who had been telling me for years that they were praying for him had their heads in their hands, weeping unashamedly.

It was late when people began to leave, and it seemed like a good time to take the kids back home. I made sure Bill had a ride back to our house when he was done talking and praying, then the kids and I walked outside into the chilly autumn night and climbed into the van. Though nothing had visibly happened to Bill, we were as expectant as children on Christmas Eve.

"What would be the first thing you'd want to do if God healed Daddy?" I asked, glancing into the rearview mirror at the kids as I drove home.

"Go camping again," Olivia yelled, "and build a fire and roast marshmallows!"

Hmm, I thought. *Nice idea, Olivia, but it would take an act of God bigger than that to get me in a tent with you again.*

Listening to the kids sharing their hearts of how their daddy's healing would affect them was exciting and scary at the same time. For all our expectation, we still didn't know what God was going to do. After we got home, most of the kids went off to bed, but Andy waited up for his dad to come home. He sat on the white wingback chair next to the window, straining to see headlights come down our street.

Soon a car pulled into the driveway and Bill got out, still holding his cane. He walked in the door and slowly climbed the stairs. I glanced over at Andy and caught him quickly wipe a tear away. Bill hobbled in and sat down on the chair next to him. "Andy, we prayed, and we know God can heal," he said, as much to reassure us as Andy. "But it's His decision, and we need to trust Him no matter what."

Bill gave Andy a hug and prayed with him before he turned and walked down the hallway to his bedroom. Years later, Andy told us he cried himself to sleep that night.

Bill and I sat for a while in the living room, talking and processing the events of the evening. The love displayed by our church was overwhelming and humbling. Both of us were emotionally spent with all that had happened, and finally decided to go to bed. Bill fell asleep quickly, but my brain kept spinning. At about 1:30 a.m. I gave up on sleep, put on my robe and tip-toed back into the living room to think and pray. Looking out our living room bay window, the outline of Mt. Rainier shone in the darkness under the moon, a silent witness to God's power and majesty.

The next morning, Bill opened his eyes, looked over at me and sat up in bed.

"Jean," he whispered, "I feel really good."

"Huh?"

"Yeah, like *really* good. I'm either having the best day I've had in three years or God has healed me."

"WHAAAAT*?!*"

Bill stood up beside the bed. So *tall!* I had forgotten how tall he was before he started using his cane. *His cane? He didn't reach for his cane!* I immediately went into control-freak mode, shooting questions at Bill.

"Should we tell the kids? Are you really healed? How will we know for sure?!"

When God heals suddenly, He doesn't typically send out text messages detailing what's just happened. O me of little faith who prayed for God to heal Bill and then didn't know what to do with myself when it appeared that He actually did!!

Bill took my hand as we sat down together on the side of the bed to pray. "Lord, please confirm to us if this is real. Even the Old Testament king, Hezekiah, asked for a sign when he was healed. And as Isaiah asked whether Hezekiah wanted God to make the sun to go backward or forward ten degrees as a sign—"[15]

I interrupted our prayer with an epiphany of sorts. "Today is the end of Daylight Savings Time and we're supposed to turn the clocks back tonight!" God in His perfect timing healed Bill the same day we turned our clocks back to standard time in the fall. However ludicrous this sounds, the similarity of our story to Hezekiah's was a confirmation to us that God truly had healed Bill, overnight, miraculously, and in answer to the prayers of many.

---

15   2 Kings 20:7-10.

The physical signs of his healing revealed themselves through the day:

No breathing problems. Check.

No pain or weakness on his left side. Check.

No difficulty swallowing. Tortilla chips going down fine. Check.

No balance problems, no need to use the cane. Check.

No slowed, foggy thinking. Bill was cracking jokes all the livelong day. Check.

Bill drove both David and Andy to their soccer games and ran up and down the sidelines, cheering them on as all the amazed parents, who knew how sick he'd been, stared at him, mouths gaping. A few of them wept tears of joy at the sight of a completely healed Bill. Andy confided to us later that he kept looking over toward the sidelines at his dad, worried he might fall down without his cane!

That afternoon, when all the soccer games were over, we stopped for pizza. After I walked into the store, Bill told me later that the kids had a conversation about us having another baby. They discussed whether the baby would be a girl or boy. *Why did their minds go there?* I wondered. I don't remember telling the kids about the vow I had made. I really don't know why they made the leap from "Dad's healed," to "Now Mom and Dad will resume their prolific childbearing ways."

But later in the week, I did remind Bill of the vow I had made. For a man who had been sick with a neuromuscular disease for three years, the opportunity to be intimate with his wife must have seemed better than winning the lotto. At least I assume that's what he was thinking! Bill and I had spent more than a year in the infirm/caregiver roles. Happily, all that changed overnight too.

Chapter 17:

CELEBRATION

The next morning was Sunday, a perfect day to celebrate with friends. We ate breakfast, got ready, hopped in the van—this time with Bill in the driver's seat—and went to church. The joy of telling people God healed Bill was beyond description. Shock, grins, tears, everyone asking, "Why don't you have your cane?!" Almost afraid to imagine that their prayers had been answered. As soon as we walked in, Priscilla, the office manager at the church, reached up to Bill and gave him a big hug that conveyed years of heartfelt prayers.

Soon after the service began the pastor asked us to come up on stage with our family to share what God had done. One of my friends who had prayed for Bill but who hadn't heard our news yet, watched him walk up the stairs without his cane and leaned over to her husband to ask, *"Where's his stick?"*

The congregation was awash in smiles and uninhibited emotion as we told them how God healed Bill miraculously, overnight. So many people praising and thanking God that He had answered *their* petitions. After the service my friend walked over to us with her 10-year-old daughter, who had asked God every night to heal Bill. Wiping away tears, she looked on as Bill hugged her little daughter to thank her for her faithful intercession. The girl's face was lit up like a child's on Christmas morning, but her gift from the Lord wasn't toys, instead it was a miraculous answer to her prayers.

The reality that this miracle was a gift, not only to us, but the entire church, made it all the more thrilling. So many people had pleaded for so long, and when God answered, it truly was for their spiritual benefit as well as for ours. Many of them still refer to it as a life-changing moment, witnessing an event showing that God still miraculously heals today. That He is *more than able* to do the supernatural. That He *hears* our prayers. It was a major faith-builder for many, many people.

Bill's healing seemed to be a faith-builder for those outside of the church too. The next week, my friend, Kim, went to the grocery store and asked the woman behind the counter in the bakery if she would personalize a cake for her.

"Sure, what would you like it to say?"

"Well, I don't think you've ever done one like this," Kim said.

"No, I've heard them all—what do you want?" she asked again.

"Happy Healing!"

"Happy *Healing?*"

"I told you you've never done one like this," Kim said, then she proceeded to share with her how God healed Bill.

The next week we went to Dr. Stewart's office to share the good news. The nurse on duty that day, a woman whom we had never met, led us into an exam room, put Bill's five-pound medical file on the counter and asked, "What brings you in to see Dr. Stewart today?"

"I need to tell him I'm healed," Bill said. The words were barely out of Bill's mouth when the nurse's eyes immediately filled with tears. *Wow, I* thought. *This woman doesn't even know us—how incredible to see God touching so many hearts with Bill's news.*

The nurse shared that she was a Christian and had visited our church in the past. She then looked down and wrote a note on Bill's chart that said "HEALED!" walked out, put the chart in the file holder on the door and went out to track down Dr. Stewart. Soon we heard some rustling out in the hall with a "What's *this?*" from Dr. Stewart. He slowly opened the door, sat down, and stared at Bill, smiling broadly while he listened to our whole story.

"Well, let's get you up here and do a quick neurological exam!"

It was no surprise to either of us when Bill was able to do everything he couldn't do at the last visit, or for the last three years, for that matter. Dr. Stewart sat back down on his stool, grinned and kept shaking his head.

"In all my years of practice, I've heard of a handful of verifiable miracles but never from one of my own patients," he said incredulously.

After a few minutes watching Dr. Stewart process this surprising turn of events, Bill asked, "So how do I get off all this medication?"

"Ah, yes. Well, let's see what you're on." Dr. Stewart scanned Bill's chart, running his finger down the list of drugs he was taking. He told Bill he could quit taking some of the medicines that day and wean off others more gradually. Then he came to the Fentanyl pain patch.

"Hmm," he said, as he raised his eyebrows. "I've never weaned anyone off of Fentanyl. When I give it to cancer patients, they usually need higher and higher doses of it, then they die. I'll have to check what the protocols are and get back to you."

(In fact, Bill came off *all* his medicine in a month. This was probably a little more of an aggressive wean than was necessary, but we were both ready to be done with all things related to his illness.) Dr. Stewart finished our time together with a promise to call our neurologist with the good news.

A few days later we went in to see the neurologist. He gave Bill a rigorous exam, then we followed him from the exam room into his office. The doctor sat behind his desk, pen in hand and stared down at Bill's file for a minute and then looked up. "So why are you better?"

"Well, we were at our church last Friday night, people prayed for me, and God healed me."

"That's great. That's great," he murmured. He scribbled some notes and then looked up again. "Is there any other administrative thing I can do for you?"

"Not that we can think of," Bill said. "Except...we do have one question...have you ever had another patient healed like this?"

"No," he said flatly. "And, if there is nothing more I can help you with, I guess I hope you come back in thirty years feeling the same way."

On the way down the stairs, Bill said, "He wasn't as enthusiastic as Dr. Stewart."

"Yeah...seemed like he wanted us out of his office," I said.

"That's fine, it's not like we're going back there anytime soon."

"They probably don't cover miraculous healing in med school."

"Ya think?" Bill said.

Reactions to our news ranged from thinly veiled skepticism to wholehearted acceptance. Surprisingly, some of the most doubtful were Christians, and some of the most accepting were not religious at all. Let's face it, when we hear claims of miraculous healing, images of wacko televangelists, snake-oil itinerant preachers, and emotional women fainting in church aisles often come to mind. But for all the skepticism our joy was not stifled. We knew people had prayed for Bill for years, as well as that night at the church. We knew God healed him. We reveled in each one of Bill's restored abilities, beyond grateful for the gift God had given us.

I feel like I'm living in a dream, and I sure don't want to wake up! This just seems so bizarre, even though I had prayed for this for so long … it's just so wonderful I can hardly believe it. We had our home Bible Study group over last night for a party, just to celebrate God's miraculous power. What a wonderful time, and what a faith-builder this is for so many. It's so much fun to hear other people's stories of who they've told, or what they felt when they found out. They all pitched in and gave us $300 to go away for the weekend! What sweet saints!
Journal, November 2, 2000

The reality of Bill's healing was an adjustment for him, me, the kids; it was mind-bending for us all. For instance, Bill kept reaching for his cane when he would get up from sitting down, and then remember he didn't need it anymore. The kids had gotten used to a dad who was in bed much of the time, in pain and not very interactive. When Bill was healed, suddenly there was a new sheriff in town, with opinions about how the kids talked to me, when they did their chores, and their whereabouts at all times. Healing wasn't all rainbows and butterflies, something they don't cover in the *Healing for Dummies* textbook. But we adjusted. As for me, I just kept asking Bill if he was still feeling okay. How like me, who likes to think that faith is my spiritual gift, to keep asking. Finally, Bill told me one day, "Look, I'm fine. God healed me." Yes. Yes, He did.

Chapter 18:

MIRACLES

People are meaning-makers and almost immediately after Bill was healed, we heard many people say things like, "Well, no one deserves this more than Bill." Their words were meant to be kind, but if that logic is followed—that Bill was healed because he deserved it—then can we also conclude that people who aren't healed *don't* deserve it?

Bill didn't *deserve* to be healed any more than anyone who isn't healed. We don't know why God chose to heal Bill. Yes, people prayed, and yes, they prayed with faith. Yet, we all know many people who pray with faith that aren't healed on this side of heaven. Rather than the focus be on Bill, the attention should be on God.

Our miracle was all about God's display of power, and His love and compassion for ordinary people like Bill. Jesus promises His church that at the end of the age, "God will wipe away every tear from their eyes; there shall be no more death, nor sorrow, nor crying. There shall be no more pain, for the former things have passed away."[16] This is our sure hope. When we do see miracles, it reminds us that very soon our faith will be sight.

However, a question we did find ourselves asking was, *why did God heal Bill and not our other friends?* When our friends who struggled with chronic illness weren't healed too, Bill and I felt an odd sense of survivor's guilt. We felt that people might think, "How can you understand what it's like to suffer from a, b or c? God *healed* you!" Did anyone say this out loud? No. It's just a sense we had and one we didn't expect. It's not like anyone's written the book on *What Happens After Being Miraculously Healed.* We just discovered this over time. Over and over. It happened when we would pray for people to be healed, and they wouldn't get healed—almost like we had lost our platform as "suffering servants." Maybe it was all in my head, but I felt it. Bill said he did too.

In addition, people began calling or emailing us and want details of how God healed Bill, like we somehow had discovered the magic formula. *How did you pray? What did you say?* But we had no prescription to offer. All we could say is that we prayed, and others prayed, and then God healed him. The bottom line is God decides where and when anyone gets healed.

God isn't bound by doing what's "fair" or doing everything the same for everyone. It's hard to hear that when someone you love is sick or dying. It's a difficult balance, praying for healing here on earth, and yet maintaining faith in God's goodness when the healing comes later, in heaven. But having a life-threatening illness demands that we shift our focus from temporary things to the eternal.

Another question circled my brain for years, and that was, *why did God do that amazing miracle at a church struggling with conflict, losing faithful members, and crumbling around questionable doctrine?* And with the clarity that time often provides, I know that compared to God's perfect understanding, our belief, obedience, and adherence to core doctrines of the Christian faith

---

16 Revelation 21:4.

is always imperfect. None of us is perfect in our understanding of doctrine—or of God. If God required us to be faultless in the way we "do church," before He healed or performed miracles, we'd *never* see them, because we are all imperfect in our orthodoxy (correct belief) and orthopraxy, (correct practice). God doesn't wait until we have perfect understanding, or go to a perfect church, or say the perfect prayer before He heals. His miraculous power touches us when He chooses, all because of His mercy and grace, never because of our merited favor.

Think of all the people in the Bible who were healed: Naaman, who wasn't a believer in God; Miriam, who was leprous because of her own sin; the ten lepers who were healed by Jesus. All these people were just like you and me, sinners in need of a healing touch by the One who stoops to our need. He doesn't wait until we're all bright, shiny, and theologically correct before He comes and rescues us. The healing should draw our attention onto Him, not onto ourselves.

God demonstrated His power and mercy that night to us and to our church. Beyond Bill's healing, or in addition to it, one thing is certain and that is our faith and trust in God grew throughout the whole trial. The faith of our friends, family members—and even strangers when they hear this story—has grown. That is one, if not the primary, goal God has in miracles: that we would "believe that He is, and that He is a rewarder of those who diligently seek Him."[17]

---

17   Hebrews 11:6.

PART 2:

ANNIE

Chapter 19:

VOW FULFILLED

Bill hadn't been planning to interview for a new job; he had been planning to die. So, when God healed him, his first thought was to return to his old job at the church. However, they'd already hired someone else to replace him because, of course, Bill was dying. And then there were the theological differences that remained between us and them, so that idea wouldn't fly. But after a few months passed and a few interviews and a decision not to move to a tiny church hidden in the woods 100 miles outside of Duluth, an executive pastor position opened at a church north of Seattle. Bill was more than anxious to be back in ministry and employed again, and as it was his pleasure and joy to provide for his family, he was thankful God had given him a second chance to do that. In May of 2001, Bill accepted the church's offer to come on staff. We were sad to say goodbye to friends in our old community, people who had walked through the valley of the shadow of death with us, but we were also anxious to begin a new chapter in life and ministry.

While Bill got acclimated to the staff and vision of our new church, I enrolled the kids at the local schools and began house-hunting. Our realtor,

James, found a house big enough for our family; one that bore a striking resemblance to our previous house. In fact, it was almost identical. After my first walk-through, I knew Bill would love it; he'd know exactly where everything was. We told James we'd take it and moved in soon after.

We settled in, did some painting, and bought a dog. Then I reminded Bill of the bargain I'd made with God, that if He healed Bill, we'd try to have another baby as a living testimony that God heals. A year or so went by, and when I didn't get pregnant, I started to get nervous. *Lord, maybe that was a stupid idea. I don't want to be 45 and pregnant.* I thought being over 40 and willingly pregnant was quite magnanimous of me. But now I was 43. Being pregnant and over 45? That would have given me hives.

So, Bill and I discussed closing up shop. Maybe he'd get a manly operation? Maybe that bargain with God was all in my head? Maybe God was happy that I'd offered it, but maybe He didn't actually expect me to follow through with it? *Besides if we went years without getting pregnant and then were surprised, well, that would be so...irresponsible,* I thought.

A few weeks later, my period was late. Bill and I were sitting together at our favorite Italian restaurant one night, and a little voice inside my head told me to opt out of my usual glass of prosecco. The waiter brought the bread and olive oil and after he left, I blurted out, "I'm late," then watched for Bill's reaction.

"You're pregnant," Bill said, calmly chewing on a piece of bread.

"Yeah, I don't know..."

"I do. You are," Bill said confidently. "We'll stop by the grocery store and pick up one of those tests on the way home."

"I am *not* going into the store for that one thing," I said.

"Then I will," he said.

We bolted our food down and scurried out of the restaurant. Bill parked in the grocery store parking lot, ran in and a few minutes later skipped out of the store with his bag of treasure. Bill always thought having a new baby was the Next.Great.Adventure, and thankfully, his enthusiasm calmed my anxiety. Now my only other concern, besides being the pregnant 43-year-old mother of seven kids, was how often I'd need to color my white hair to disguise the fact that technically, I *could* be knitting booties for my grandchildren.

After we got home from the store, the first test was positive, as was the second. I didn't try for a third.

So here we are...I'm 43, Bill's almost 44, and we're pregnant with baby number seven. And true to my promise in my journal of March 8, 2000, in which I said that if God healed Bill, I'd try to have a baby and name him Josiah, which means "God heals," if we do have a boy, his name will be Josiah. But if it's a girl, I don't know what her name will be. What is a girl's name that means "God heals"? Journal, August 3, 2002

Being pregnant for me was like riding a bike. I knew the drill. First order of business: make an appointment with the obstetrician. Since we had moved back to the area where two of our other children, Andy and David, were born, I called the office of the doctor who delivered them.

"He's *retired??*" I asked incredulously.

"Yes, he's here, but he doesn't deliver babies anymore," said the receptionist.

Well, I started counting my fingers and remembered it *had* been fifteen years since Andy's birth, and thirteen years since David's.

"Oh, don't feel bad," the doctor said as we chatted in his office a couple of weeks later. "My oldest patient was 49 and pregnant with her tenth child." His attempt at assuaging my doubts wasn't working. I thought of all the elderly women in the Bible who had kids late in life. It was little consolation that at least I wasn't 90 like Abraham's wife, Sarah.

"Well, who else delivers babies at this hospital?" I asked him. "Anyone who can shave?"

"I'll refer you to another doctor in our group. You'll like him."

A few months later, we scheduled an appointment that included an ultrasound to screen for any genetic abnormalities common to premeno-pausal pregnant women. (Not that we'd have changed course had anything been found.) My goal was simply to find out what color we were having, blue or pink. Bill and I watched the screen while the ultrasound technician searched for life under globs of silicone slime.

"Ah, there we go, do you see? There's the heart...looks good, four healthy chambers...and a leg, and..."

"It's a girl!" Bill interrupted.

"Good call, Dad," the tech said.

"Yes, I've seen five boys and I guessed our last one, a girl. It's a girl, alright." Bill nodded confidently. The little peanut was squirming around, opening and closing her mouth, putting her hand over her face and roll-ing around.

"Bless her heart," I said, feeling a tear roll into my ear. All babies are miracles, and this one, especially, to all of us. Olivia, in particular, was thrilled to have a sister to balance out the testosterone in our tribe.

In the spring, about a month before her due date, my friend, Cindy, from our church hosted a lovely baby shower for us, with pink tulips, pink frosted cookies, and enough pink outfits and pink baby gear to last until she could drive. Even the trees outside were decorated with clouds of pink blossoms. Everything was working in concert to welcome this new Sullivan baby girl into the world.

After a few false starts, the doctor scheduled me to be induced on April 7, 2003. Apparently, doctors don't like to induce nowadays, but I don't like surprises, and babies by appointment had always worked well for me in the past. I wanted to know the gender and the day they'd arrive. If the doctor had that information, I needed it too.

The day finally arrived, and Annalee Grace Sullivan took her first breath at 3:36 p.m. She weighed in at 8 lbs.11 oz., and measured 21 1/2 inches long. Healthy, beautiful, with light blond hair and ten fingers and ten toes. Her brothers and sister were delighted—not to mention Bill and me. Bill changed her name as he was filling out the birth certificate at the hospital. "Why don't we make Anna Lee one name, "Annalee," and give her "Grace" as a middle name? Because it's by God's grace she was even conceived," he said.

Annie, as we called her, was a double grace—*grace upon grace*, for us. The name Ann, which also means grace, was in honor of my mom, and "Lee," after my sister Rebecca's middle name, seemed a good fit, meaning "sheltered from the storm."

Annie grew like a weed, or a Sullivan, and by the time she was four months old, people would regularly comment on how *tall* she was. How an infant could be tall I didn't know, but we heard it over and over again. She also established herself as a capital-E extrovert. When I put her in the front pack facing out, she'd kick her legs and arms in a bid to lure anyone into a conversation. Annie was our little lemur baby, with big round eyes which grew even rounder when she was drowsy and ready for a nap.

By the time she was a year old, Annie was standing next to furniture, drinking from a cup, and achieving the usual milestones. All of them, that is, except walking. When she was 15 months old and still not walking I started to be concerned. But when her siblings left to go to summer camp one week and weren't around to carry her where she wanted to go, that's when Annie decided to walk.

Annie has grown by leaps and bounds and now has decided to climb up on everything. She talks constantly and her favorite phrase is "Go away!" She says it to big brothers who scare her, tease her or pick her up when she wants to be down. She says "T-tales" when she wants someone to turn on her Veggie Tale movie. "Up-up-up" when she wants out of her crib, "Eat!" when she's hungry. She is an extrovert D-type personality I think.

She was talking to her Raggedy Ann doll while I changed her diaper today. "Eyes, nose, eyes, nose," she'd point to her doll's eyes and then point to her own eyes, "Eyes, eyes." Then point to her doll's nose, then her own, "Nose, nose." She talks about everything! Journal, January 6, 2005

Annie loved for us to read to her. *What Does God Do?* by Hans Wilhelm was a favorite book, with pictures of cherubs acting out scenes in the Bible: angels holding up the sun and moon in the Creation story, angels sliding down a rainbow beside the animals of the ark. Every time I'd sit down to read it to her, Annie would repeat the same questions for each page. On the last page, a little baby is wrapped with a snuggly blanket inside a cradle, with the verse, "You made me in an amazing and wonderful way. All the days planned for me were written in Your book before I was one day old."[18]

She'd always pointed to the baby in the cradle and ask, "Is that me, Mommy?"

"Yep, that's you," I'd say.

Okay, so the baby in the picture wasn't *exactly* Annie ... but she *had* been a baby. And God *had* planned all her days before she was one day old.

---

18   Psalm 139:14, 16, (NCV).

Chapter 20:

FIRST CRISIS

Because Annie was our little caboose, I treasured every stage of her infancy and toddlerhood. Didn't want to let them go, to be honest. Having had six other children, I knew the warp speed at which children grow up and savored each moment with her. I didn't even put Annie in the complimentary babysitting area of the local grocery store because I loved to listen to her chatter while she rode in the giant car grocery cart up and down the aisles.

During the spring and summer months, Annie followed me around our backyard garden with her pink garden trowel and shovel, tip-toeing along the gravel paths that bordered the flower beds. After she turned two, I noticed her skin seemed to tan more easily than my other kids and seemed to stay darker in the fall after the weather changed. The creases on her finger and toe knuckles were dark, too. Annie's skin had a distinct golden glow. It came on slowly, almost imperceptibly, and I attributed it to the genes from Bill's side of the family, because his dad had an olive skin tone. I really didn't give it much thought. It never occurred to me that her bronze skin color could be a symptom of a disease. Then at the end of December, Annie came down with a virus.

Annie's still sick. The fever is gone, but she is barely keeping sips of water and apple juice down. She does the dry heaving thing—last time around 8 p.m. But now she's asleep after a sip of water and two sips of apple juice. She had a wet pull-up and she also tinkled in the potty chair just now, so I guess she's not too dehydrated, but she looks it. I am so worried about her. Lord, please heal her tonight. Heal her vomiting problem and give her Your touch of health. She needs to turn a corner tonight. I really hope no one else gets this virus, or whatever it is, from Annie. Journal, December 31, 2005

None of my other six kids had ever been this sick and they'd had just about every childhood illness in the book. I kept waiting for Annie to recover like the other kids always did. But it wasn't happening. Early on New Year's Day morning, I bundled her up, carried her to the van and sped down the freeway to the hospital. By the time I got her there she was limp and not responding to any questions. I gave the nurse a brief history, and he quickly gathered supplies to start an IV, but her veins were flat from dehydration. The sweat beaded on the ER nurse's forehead as he tried repeatedly to get an IV into Annie's veins. She lay there, pale, eyes closed and completely unresponsive to the needle sticks. *Dear God, help us. Help him. Heal Annie. Save Annie,* I pleaded, overwhelmed with fear and guilt that I had waited too long to get help.

Another nurse, a young woman from our church, was working that morning and paced the hallway outside our exam room. I knew she was praying. Then someone checked Annie's blood glucose level—a critically low 14—and that's when the doctor started yelling. *"We need to get sugar into her or she's going to seize!"*

The room instantly filled with technicians, nurses, doctors, everyone rushing around to save Annie's life. A normal blood glucose level is 70–100. Below 40, 30 or even 20, brings a decreasing level of mental function, leading to unconsciousness, seizures, coma and death. Annie was gravely ill, and she needed sugar in her body *now*. Someone came running with packets of honey, and the doctor tore them open and squirted them into the sides of Annie's mouth. Then an ambulance was called to transport her to the more specialized Children's Hospital.

"They're experts with kids down there; they'll be able to get an IV into her," the doctor assured me. I wondered if there was enough time—Children's was at least 15-20 minutes away with no traffic. The medics appeared and quickly rolled Annie's gurney into the ambulance. I sat up front with the driver. He turned on the lights and sirens and pulled up to Children's Emergency Department in 15 minutes flat.

We were met by the resuscitation team who feverishly worked on getting an IV into her, but they found the same dehydrated veins. Another glucose test registered 20, up six points, no doubt from the honey pooling in her mouth. They decided to place an I.O.—Intraosseous infusion—an IV into Annie's right leg bone, a couple of inches below her knee. An I.O. provides emergency fluids and medications directly into the leg bone when IV access is not feasible.[19]

Bill met me at the hospital and we stood together, just outside of the circle of the medical staff surrounding Annie. We prayed as we watched, barely breathing, tied up in knots at the sight of them fighting for Annie's life. As soon as the I.O. was placed, the nurses got another IV into her left hand. Her face was covered with an oxygen mask, and the head of the gurney was tipped back so gravity would help blood get to her brain. Everyone worked quietly, whispering status updates unintelligible to hysterical parents. Relief flooded into the room as the IV glucose and sodium fluids flowed into her veins, bringing her back from the brink.

I can't remember when Annie woke up, in the ER or in the room she where was admitted. But by the end of her second day in the hospital, the I.O. was removed from her thin little leg and a bandage placed over the bruise.

---

19   http://emedicine.medscape.com/article/908610-overview.

The fluids had re-inflated her, swelling her eyes almost shut. She lay in her hospital bed, no strength to get up and around, clutching her favorite pink and blue rag blanket with one hand and her Raggedy Ann doll with the other.

The next morning, after being poked and analyzed by a parade of technicians and phlebotomists, Annie asked for some goldfish crackers and devoured one snack-size bag of them before falling back asleep. As I watched her napping, I felt the prayers of my family and friends. My thoughts were interrupted when the doctor walked in and announced that Annie had tested positive for rotavirus, a common childhood illness. I stood on the other side of Annie's bed and asked, "Are you *sure* that's all it was? Our six other kids must have had rotavirus, too, and they never got this sick."

The doctor waved me off and said, "Oh, yes, it's not unusual for kids to get very sick with rotavirus."

It seemed as if the doctor didn't quite comprehend the seriousness of how sick Annie had been. Like when you've been in a near-fatal car accident where you almost died but didn't. You tell your friends all about it, but they see you're fine now, so they don't realize how bad it was.

When I was nineteen, a semi-tractor trailer clipped the driver's side rear wheel well of the car I was driving, my mother's brand-new Toyota Corolla. The impact swung my car directly into the front of the semi so that I was, in effect, being pushed up the freeway. I looked to my left and stared into the grill of the white Freightliner for a moment, then my car suddenly spun away from the truck and into on-coming traffic. I watched the other drivers frantically trying to avoid me—eyes wide, brakes slamming, cars fishtailing. My car kept spinning until it was about to hit the concrete median, and then suddenly spun the other way. It finally stopped just off the right side of the freeway, pointing in the right direction. My hand trembled as I turned off the radio. "Thank You, Lord, that I am still alive," I said out loud.

I opened my door as another truck driver who stopped to help walked up to me.

"Are you okay?" he asked.

"Yeah, I think so," I said.

"Man, I thought you were going to lose it there a few times. I can't believe you didn't roll!"

"Yeah, me either." I was shaking uncontrollably as I surveyed the damage to my mother's car. The entire left side was crunched, and the front bumper bent, scraping on the tires. A California highway patrolman pulled over to take a report and instructed me to get my car off the freeway. He thought the car was drivable, and his top priority was maintaining the flow of traffic on his freeway, my near-death experience was not.

Here in the hospital, Annie looked fine, but she had been so close to dying. I wanted to believe that rotavirus was the cause of Annie's crisis, but in the back of my mind I felt something else was going on. *None of my kids ever were as sick as Annie,* I thought. *But I wasn't the doctor; what did I know?*

Chapter 21:

TROUBLE BREWING

A few days after we got home from the hospital Annie still couldn't walk by herself. I counted fourteen pokes on her arms, legs and feet. One of them was a blood draw, three were IV sites, but the rest were from the nurses trying unsuccessfully to get an IV into her. I didn't even count the pin pricks on the ends of her fingers from blood glucose checks. Annie went through so much pain to get rehydrated, and I felt so guilty for not taking her in sooner. That night, I tucked her and Olivia into bed. Annie was still cranky and teary-eyed. *I remember being depressed after being sick when I was a kid,* I thought. *Lord, help me to be a more diligent and wise mother. Thank You again for saving Annie's life. Please continue to strengthen and heal her.*

Annie took quite a long time to recover, slowly regaining her strength. Throughout the next year, each time she'd get any sort of bug, the dark circles under her eyes would reappear giving her a gaunt and dehydrated look. Bill and I were not about to repeat her emergency of January, so if she got the least bit sick we wasted no time in taking her to the doctor's office.

That summer Annie seemed almost back to her old self, skipping over our gravel paths in the garden, digging with her garden tools, and holding the hose while I gave the flowers a drink. Many evenings that summer, our family gathered around the backyard fire pit and roasted s'mores, while Annie would plead for as many "marsh-lellows" as she could get. When the sky grew dark and it was time for bed, I'd pick her up and climb the stairs up to the deck, pausing for a moment so she could look up at the stars and try to make out the constellations. Every ordinary activity seemed precious through Annie's 3-year-old eyes.

One day in August, Annie said her tummy hurt and she felt like she was going to throw up. Bill and I took her down to our family doctor's office to check for appendicitis. David had appendicitis when he was 7 years old, and I thought Annie's symptoms were very similar to his, but the X-ray ruled it out. So, we left to go home. Annie was still complaining of stomach pain, though, and because I couldn't shake the feeling something was wrong, we drove down to Children's Hospital for a second opinion. When we arrived, I lifted Annie out of the van, and wondered if I should take her pink, plastic bin we had from the previous hospital visit in with us, just in case she needed to throw up in the waiting room. "They'll have something in there if she needs it," Bill said. "Let's just go in."

When we got through triage and into an exam room, the doctor looked Annie over and decided she didn't need anything that Gatorade and a snack of goldfish crackers wouldn't fix. I always questioned myself when I'd take her into the doctors or ER, especially when they found "nothing" wrong with her. "Oh, kids get dehydrated," they'd say. *Was I being a hypochondriac with my kid? Was I overreacting?* I'd ask myself. Then I'd remember her limp body in the ER in January. *No, something is wrong. And even if they think I'm a loon, I won't let that happen again.*

I noticed the creases on her fingers and toes were darker, and the overall tone of her skin became even more golden. The color made her hands look dirty sometimes. Once I decided to scrub them, trying to get them clean, and felt awful when Annie looked up at me as if I was hurting her. Other people noticed her tanned skin color too. A gal who worked in the church office started calling Annie, "Malibu Barbie."

It was around that time I went to the grocery store with Annie, and as I walked across the parking lot holding her tanned hand in mine, a voice in my head warned, *Enjoy the soft little hand in yours, because this time won't last forever.* I pushed the thought back and wondered why I was being so melodramatic.

Bill and I celebrated our 25th wedding anniversary in September with a trip to Ireland, a generous surprise gift from our church family. Bill's ancestors are from the Republic of Ireland, and my grandfather was born in Belfast, so we had both sides of the family to dig up. We made arrangements for friends to stay at our house with our school-age children while we were gone. Annie wasn't in school yet, so she stayed part of the time with Cindy, the Church Office Manager, and Vickie, the Children's Pastor. Annie spent many hours at Vickie's house as a toddler, almost becoming like one of her other children. Vickie and her husband, Jack, had older kids the same age as our older ones, and they both enjoyed hosting our little caboose often. Bill and I knew Annie and the kids were in capable hands, so we left for Ireland looking forward to some relaxing time alone.

We flew into Shannon Airport on the west side of the Republic, rented a car and took an eight-day loop around the island on the wrong side of the road, probably the first real test of our 25-year union. We shared country lanes, or more accurately farm paths, with bicyclists, sheep and tour buses, often all at the same time. Pity the hapless farmer crossing the road during busy daylight hours. Occasionally I'd peek through my fingers to catch a glimpse of rolling green turf dotted with ancient castles, breathtaking sights, my hyperventilating notwithstanding. We stopped at a few old graveyards and saw Scripture verses written on the tombstones of saints from centuries past. *How the family of God is linked from generation to generation,* I mused. *Our roots are in Ireland, both physical and spiritual.*

About halfway through our trip, I called home because I missed my kids so much. I found out that Annie had come down with a urinary tract infection that necessitated a trip to the doctor. Cindy took her, got the antibiotics and assured me that all was well.

But dang, I miss my little girl and want to go home and take care of her! Lord, please watch over all my kids and keep them healthy and safe. Ditto for us...and make this time go by fast so we can all be together again. Journal, September 16, 2006

Bill and I continued our route from Galway, north to Sligo and then onto Belleek, where we stopped at the factory where they make the delicate ivory-colored china with little shamrocks which I'd collected since before we were married. Then we drove east to Belfast, south to Dublin, and cut back through the middle of the island to Kilkenny and south to the coast to Kinsale. Then back up to the Shannon Airport and onto a plane bound for home. We loved Ireland and hope to return again someday. But going home meant I could quit worrying about Annie.

When we got home, we heard that Annie required a different antibiotic after breaking out in hives from a reaction to the first. While she was recovering, Cindy handed her off to Vickie who knew Annie was feeling better when she wanted to take a bubble bath in Miss Vickie's whirlpool tub, complete with her favorite bedtime story, *The Napping House*. Vickie told me later they read it so often that Annie would complete the sentences of the story for her. I was so grateful for Cindy and Vickie tag teaming on Annie's care and was relieved to be home with the kids after being gone. Relieved to be driving on the right side of the road as well.

Chapter 22:

LIFE WITH ANNIE

Annie nailed the role of spoiled little sister and provided hours of entertainment for her siblings. Her favorite game with older brother, David, was called Slug Bug. When we ran errands around town in our van, the first person to see a yellow Volkswagen Bug yelled "My slug bug!" David usually saw the yellow Volkswagen first, and quickly laid claim to it, provoking loud protests from his little sister. "That's *my* slug bug, *I wanted* that slug bug!!" Annie pouted. Her meltdowns made David laugh, which stirred her pot even more.

"I'm not your friend!" Annie glared.

"Oh, really?"

"That was *my* slug bug!"

Then another yellow Volkswagen Bug would appear. "My slug bug," David teased.

By the age of three, I thought Annie should be learning to share, play fairly, and perhaps move out of the annoying little sister stage. *Maybe board games would help her learn fair play,* I thought.

"Let's play CandyLand," I suggested one afternoon.

"I love CandyLand! I want to be Queen Frostine," Annie said.

"We'll just have to see who lands on her," I said.

I got the game down from the closet, laid the board on the table along with the cards and the little gingerbread men. Then I made the fatal mistake of landing on Queen Frostine.

"I wanted to be QUEEN FROST-*TEEN*!!!" Annie screamed, as water squirted from every orifice of her face. *This is going to be harder than I thought,* I thought to myself.

Royalty must've been in her genes, because besides wanting to be Queen Frostine, she was convinced she was a princess. We gave her a blond-haired Cinderella doll for Christmas one year, complete with a blue dress and painted on eyelashes. Annie carried that Cinderella doll around with her everywhere, and in her bedroom when no one was looking, she decorated the blue dress with pink magic marker. At some point, she decided her name needed to be changed. "My name isn't Annie, it's Cinderella—la!"

Annie memorized songs and Bible verses easily, and each day we'd work through verses corresponding to the alphabet:

"A is for All. For all have sinned and fall short of the glory of God."

"B is for Believe. Believe on the Lord Jesus Christ and you shall be saved."

"C is for Children. Children obey your parents."

By the end of 2006, Annie had memorized all the way up to "K is for Keep—Keep your tongue from evil and your lips from speaking lies." It didn't take her long to discover that verses were useful to browbeat her siblings into submission at the breakfast table.

"It's morning time!" Annie announced one day as she pushed off the covers, climbed out of the bottom bunkbed and walked down the hall toward the kitchen. "Can I have some marsh-lellow cereal for bref-kiss?" Marshmallow Mateys was her favorite cereal, and she'd typically eat all the marshmallow bits and then leave the oat pieces floating in the bowl. Olivia was the one pouring her cereal that morning and when Annie wanted more cereal, she said, "No, Annie, you need to eat what's in your bowl first."

Annie frowned. "Children, obey your Pear-ants!"

"You're not my parent, Annie," Olivia explained.

"Hmpf. I'm not your friend," Annie said, folding her arms and glaring sideways at her big sister.

Another time, we all sat down to dinner with Annie in her highchair next to Bill, and our six other kids lined up along both sides of the table. Annie kept dithering her father for more tortilla chips.

"No, Annie," Bill said.

She didn't like that answer, so she asked again.

"Annie, I told you no," her daddy said once more.

Annie frowned at him, looked at me, then made her last pitch.

"I was talking to *Mom*," she said.

Obviously, Annie's memorized Bible verses didn't automatically equate to godly behavior. But she *was* only three, I reminded myself. The good news was she often asked deep spiritual questions, almost as if there wasn't enough time for her to get all the answers she needed. One morning Annie leaned against the bathroom door as she watched me put on makeup for the day, and asked, "Mommy, how can the Holy Spirit be in your heart and in heaven at the same time?" *Huh?* I thought. *How was I supposed to explain abstract truth to a 3-and-a-half-year old?* She wanted to know things I could barely wrap *my* head around. "Well, God is everywhere," I said. "His Spirit can be in both places at the same time." Satisfied with my answer, Annie turned around and skipped away, blond curls swinging behind her.

Chapter 23:

THE APPROACHING STORM

I n October, our church's annual women's retreat was held in La Conner, a picturesque fishing village in the Skagit Valley, half-way between Seattle and the Canadian border. It's a touristy chick sort of town, a place Bill loathes but will endure visiting for my birthday or an anniversary. The women's ministry team booked the La Conner Country Inn for our retreat, complete with cozy fireplaces in each room, and overstuffed chairs in the lobby to relax with a mug of hot chocolate.

"Finding Your Story in His Story," was the title of the talk I gave, a study in the Old Testament book of Ruth. In this story, Ruth, and her mother-in-law, Naomi, are the main characters. Naomi's husband and two grown sons (one of whom was married to Ruth) all died within a ten-year span, leaving both women widows with no visible means of support. Naomi's response to these losses? Bitterness. She concluded that God must be against her. "Do not call me Naomi," she said to her friends, but "Call me Mara," or *bitter*, "for the Almighty has dealt very bitterly with me."[20]

Naomi's losses piled up: no husband, no sons, no prospect of grand-children to carry on the family name, no Social Security, no life insurance, no money, no nothing. Her future did, indeed, look hopeless. Naomi urged her daughter-in-law, Ruth, to go find another husband, but Ruth insisted on hanging with Naomi no matter what. "Entreat me not to leave you, *or to turn back from following after you;* For wherever you go, I will go; And wherever you lodge, I will lodge; Your people *shall* be my people, And your God, my God."[21]

Naomi soon discovered that God wasn't against her as she had sup-posed, but providentially provided for them through the kindness of a near relative, or *kinsman.* This *kinsman redeemer,* Boaz, eventually married Ruth and took his new mother-in-law, Naomi, into his household too. What Naomi thought was hopeless became hope-*filled.* In time, Ruth and Boaz had a son, Obed, who eventually became the grandfather to King David, the ancestor of our Kinsman Redeemer, Jesus Christ. Naomi's hopeless situation was redeemed, or 'bought back,' through the kindness of Boaz. Boaz was a type of Christ, or a foreshadowing of how Jesus became our Redeemer by dying on the cross to pay for our sins and buy back our lives that were lost.

I asked the women at the retreat to consider their stories in light of the story God is writing, and trust that He can redeem even our most bitter loss. I wanted them to trust God for their losses, as Bill and I learned to do through his illness. Our situation looked hopeless when Bill was sick, but God healed him and redeemed our trials, even giving us another child, Annie. Ruth, Naomi and I had much in common that way. I liked the way our stories mirrored each other, and I thought our story of loss and God's

---

20   Ruth 1:20. (NKJ)

21   Ibid, 16.

redemption was pretty much written. After our retreat, I returned home and looked forward to the changing seasons and upcoming holidays.

The first day of November dawned cold, crisp, and sunny; perfect for raking the leaves of the massive maple that towered over our front yard. Annie helped me by pushing the leaves around with her rake, which was twice as big as she. Her little 3-year-old voice, insistent that she could do it *all by herself,* was always a source of joy and amusement for our family. *How blessed we are to have this little blond waif,* I thought, as I packed the big, green yard waste bin with leaves. Annie trotted behind me as I rolled it out to the end of our driveway. The trash guys were scheduled to pick it up the next day, just before the forecasted rain and wind blew in that weekend. Any leaf left hanging by a thread on the old maple tree would soon fly away.

By early December most of my Christmas shopping was done, and all that remained to do was bake some cookies. Annie liked to help me mix the batter with the wooden spoon and then insisted on testing whatever came out of the oven. With my other kids moving into and beyond their teen years, I knew this was my last chance to enjoy this stage one more time. I put on Annie's favorite *Charlie Brown Christmas* music, and while I worked at the kitchen counter, Annie swung open the pantry door and hid behind it. The door was her make-believe entrance to a grocery store or kitchen or whatever her mind thought up that day. If I closed it, she'd frown and open it up again. Her antics kept me entertained until all the baking was done.

In mid-December after putting Annie down for a nap, I stood at the kitchen window and looked out into the garden. The sky above the trees grew ominous with an approaching storm. Just before it came full force, there was a light shower and then the sun shone bright against the dark clouds. A luminous rainbow appeared across the sky: *God's promise to never flood the earth again,* I thought. The Holy Spirit brought to my mind the verse in 2 Peter 1:3-4: "His divine power has given to us all things pertaining to life and godliness, through the knowledge of Him who called us to His own glory and excellence, by which He has granted to us exceedingly great and precious promises..."

He's given us everything we need, and promises to help us live like He did, I thought. *We have a powerful God who keeps His promises.* I looked up at the sky again. The clouds were black, which made the rainbow that much more brilliant. *But why did the verses in 2 Peter come to mind that afternoon?* I wondered. *That God has given me everything I need to live a godly life, and given me great and precious promises...why?* It wasn't long before I realized that He was promising me that He'd be with me in the approaching storm. I just had no idea of how black and dark it would be.

The next day we had the most powerful windstorm we'd had in over a dozen years. Electricty was out for the better part of a day; many people in the area were without power for a week. The day after the windstorm Annie came down with another stomach-flu bug. She got sick on Tuesday, threw up Wednesday afternoon, then threw up again Friday night. Bill and I took her down to the ER again, which we always did after her crisis the previous January. What was causing all these downward spirals? Why didn't she bounce back like my other kids always did? Annie just seemed so sick. I was beside myself with fear that she might repeat the crisis of the previous January.

"What's going on with Annie?" the nurse asked, as she wrote on her clipboard.

"This is our third time down here this year," I said.

"Really?" she said as she took notes.

"Yes, she gets much sicker, much faster, than any of our other kids."

"When has she been down here before?" she asked, as she continued writing.

"Well in January Annie was so dehydrated, they put an I.O. into her leg bone and she was inpatient for three days. Then we came down in August because she was nauseated and had stomach pain. Now it's December and she keeps having these episodes of nausea, vomiting—she's just so sick."

"We need to figure out why this keeps happening," Bill insisted.

"Let me share this information with the doctor," the nurse said as she left the room.

The doctor came back in a few minutes later. "Kids can get really dehydrated when they're sick," the doctor said. So they ordered an IV to rehydrate her.

A little while later, the doctor came back and said, "She seems to be better now with the fluids. You should schedule a follow-up visit with her pediatrician this week."

A couple of days later, I took Annie in to see our family doctor. "Look, I don't know what's wrong with her, but *something* is. She needs to have some tests run," I told him. What tests, I didn't know. In the back of my mind, I was wondering if she had leukemia. Kids with leukemia get sick often. My mother died of it. I knew leukemia could masquerade as unexplained illnesses before it showed its true colors. The doctor offered to do a complete panel of blood tests but seemed to question my concerns because Annie wasn't in any dire circumstance right then. She looked fine sitting there in the office. Maybe he thought I was being a hypochondriac mother. For myself, I was fighting against my tendency to doubt myself and not question the doctor—*after all, he's the authority, right? Doctors know best, don't they?*

A few days later I called the office to find out the results of Annie's blood tests. They said her tests appeared to be normal. *Normal? Well, that's a relief,* I thought. *At least she doesn't have leukemia.* That's what I thought, *at least she doesn't have leukemia,* because after all, the blood tests were normal. But I still couldn't shake the feeling something was wrong. The doctors had all checked her out. The blood tests were normal, weren't they? Yet in her Christmas pictures, Annie's skin was a dark golden color. Her pajamas hung on her. She was gaunt and skinny. Something wasn't right.

Chapter 24:

BRAIN INJURY

On the morning of Thursday, January 18, I taught a Bible study to a group of women at our church. It was a gathering of older and younger moms who met every other week to study and encourage each other in our roles as wives and mothers.

In the book of John, when Jesus' friend Lazarus was sick and near death, his sisters sent word to Jesus to come and heal him. Instead of coming right away, Jesus stayed two more days in the town where he was, and during that time, Lazarus died. When Jesus finally did come, Lazarus' sister Martha said, "Lord, if You would have been here, my brother wouldn't have died."[22]

I asked the women if they'd ever experienced a crisis and thought,

"Lord—if You'd have been here, this wouldn't have happened."

"Lord—if You'd have been here, it would be different."

"Lord—where are You??"

---

22 John 11:21.

We talked about how Jesus didn't get offended by Martha's frustrated comment, but gently redirected her and said: *"I am the resurrection and the life: he who believes in Me, though he were dead, yet shall he live. Do you believe this?"* [23] Martha said yes, she believed, even though she was probably wondering where He was going with the conversation. That is, she wondered until Jesus raised Lazarus from the dead. I reminded the ladies that whether healing comes in this life, like Lazarus, or in the next, in heaven, God's plan is good, and we can trust Him with our lives and the lives of our children.

After class, I went downstairs to retrieve Annie from her classroom. She loved her teachers, Joy and Lori, and usually balked at having to leave. After I zipped up her coat and she hugged her teachers, we walked down the hallway and out the double doors into the brisk winter air.

Three days later, very early on a Sunday morning, I woke up to 11-year-old Olivia standing over my bed. "Mommy! Annie needs you…I think she needs a tissue." I looked at the clock on my nightstand—5:15 a.m.—then pushed off the covers, got up and met Olivia in the hallway. Flipping on the hallway light I asked, "What's the matter? Is everything okay?"

Annie had been fighting a little cold. I put her to bed the night before after she ate a few nibbles of a bacon and egg dinner. Bacon was really all she'd eaten. I gave her some kid's cold medicine, tucked her in, listened to her prayers, kissed her, then turned on the humidifier and closed the door.

I followed Olivia into their darkened room, and a sliver of light shone over Annie's blond head. Suddenly, I heard her *choking? Or was she gurgling?*

Oh my God, I thought, *what is she choking on?* Kneeling beside her bed, I turned her toward me. "Annie?" No response. I touched her face in the darkness and felt more than saw that her pillow was wet, covered in vomit. Scooping up her body, her legs dangling lifelessly, I screamed, "Bill! Bill, BILL wake up!" as I ran with her into the living room and laid her on

---

23 Ibid. 25-26.

the floor to begin CPR. Bill stumbled out of our bedroom, quickly surveyed the catastrophe unfolding before his eyes and dialed 911.

"Yes, it's my daughter—she's not breathing. She's three. I don't know—I think she's choking on something!"

Annie's teeth were clenched, her pinprick pupils stared straight ahead, her fists were drawn up inward to her chest, her face was skeletal. I knew from reading my mother's old nursing school textbooks that arm posturing was a sign of severe brain injury. *But why—why was this happening to Annie? Dear God—what is going on?*

The 911 dispatcher coached Bill who in turn told me what to do. "Jean, swipe her mouth and see if there's anything in there." I tried to pry open Annie's jaw, but it was locked tight. I pushed my finger into her little mouth but found nothing. "There's nothing—Please don't die Annie, please don't die," I pleaded out loud. In my heart, I knew her brain was being ruined—it was ruined—her brain was dying. Annie was dying right in front of me, and I didn't know why.

"Jean, blow into her mouth and nose twice, then give her thirty chest compressions!" Bill instructed. "One-two-three-four-five..." I started to count. After the compressions, we listened to her. She was barely breathing, but the 911 operator told us we could stop giving her compressions and stop breathing for her.

Our sons were up out of bed with all the noise and paced about in the living room. Peter hurried outside to wait for the ambulance and waved the medics in as soon as they parked in front of our house. They clambered up the stairs with all their gear while Bill quickly relayed to them what we had been doing to try to help her.

"Could she have gotten into any drugs or medicine?" the medic asked Bill.

"No—she was asleep in her bed—"

"Has she ever had a seizure?"

"No!"

The medics quickly placed an oxygen mask on Annie, assessed her vital signs, and began administering rescue IVs of what, I didn't know. I went around the corner into the kitchen, not being able to bear the sight of how Annie looked. She looked like death. The overwhelming finality of the devastation of Annie's body and brain, her limp legs, the *enormity* of it—somehow I knew that the bright, precocious Annie I had put to bed the night before was forever gone. My vision and awareness tunneled into a circle directly in front of me. I couldn't hear what anyone was saying. All I knew was that whatever damage was done in Annie's brain was horribly permanent. I was shaking. My mind was consumed with questions. *What caused this nightmare? Why is this happening?*

The medics explained that Annie was in status epilepticus—having continuous seizures. They prepared to transport her to Children's Hospital and said I could go in the ambulance with her. Bill told me to get dressed, but in my shock-like state, taking precious seconds to put on appropriate clothing seemed like a waste of time. I walked outside in the dark, cold January morning in my old, pink bathrobe and climbed into the front seat of the ambulance. "Jesus, Jesus, Jesus," I couldn't put thoughts together to pray, but kept whispering *"Jesus, help, help, help, help!"*

This circle of hell made no sense to me. *What caused this? What was happening inside her body?* I remembered the doctor yelling in the ER the year before that if we didn't get honey into Annie's mouth she would seize. Was this seizure also caused by low blood sugar? But this time, her crisis happened in the middle of the night when we were sleeping. We didn't see her descent into unconsciousness and seizures. It happened at night. We didn't know she needed us. Olivia heard her gurgling, she thought she needed a tissue. And she got up and got me. Olivia got up and rescued her little sister.

The ambulance driver flipped on the lights and sirens. We sped down the freeway; the few cars out early that morning steered to the shoulder to make way for us. The ambulance inside was silent except for the muffled voices of the paramedics in the back working on Annie.

"How do you think she's doing?" I asked the driver.

"I'm not sure." He looked in his rearview mirror at the medics working on Annie, then glanced over at me. "You seem pretty calm for what's going on."

I thought he was kidding. It must have been the peace or grace God was giving me at that moment, at least externally. Internally, I was tied up in a strangling knot.

"I know God can heal her," I said, trying to convince myself. "God healed my husband, and I know He can heal Annie." I proceeded to fill up the silence of the ambulance with the story of Bill's healing. It was the only thing giving me hope.

The driver was moved by Bill's story, but both of us knew Annie was gravely ill and might not make it to the hospital. I turned around and looked through the window into the back, trying to read the guarded expressions on the medics working on Annie. So far, they hadn't given up, so I had hope.

We arrived at Children's Emergency Department and the medics whisked Annie into the same room she'd been in almost exactly a year before. Bill walked in with me, after following the ambulance down the freeway in his car. The resuscitation room was large enough for the gurney Annie was on, and the team of about ten medical staff surrounding her. Additional staff scurried in and out through the large doorway. I sat on a faded, pink vinyl recliner while Bill paced. I looked at the clock: 6 a.m.

The nurses couldn't get an IV into Annie because she was so dehydrated, just like the year before. They prepped her for an I.O., a needle bored into her leg to deliver lifesaving fluids, just like the year before. Bill overheard one of the doctors who was reading Annie's records whisper, "She's had an I.O. before, and *we were the ones who gave it to her.*"

Annie was pale, her eyes were closed, and she was totally unresponsive. The staff tilted the head of the gurney down so gravity would force lifesaving blood into her brain. Quiet and efficient nurses took turns manually bagging her, forcing oxygen into Annie's lungs. Soon, she no longer looked skeletal, but relaxed and pink again. Bill and I tried to overhear what the doctors and nurses were saying, but their hushed tones and guarded faces spoke loud enough. Rick, an elder at our church and a policeman, appeared and stood silently beside us. His calm presence reminded me that God was there too.

The kids at home told us later that they went to church that morning, instinctively knowing they needed to be around people who would comfort them. Our church family gathered around them, hugged and prayed for them. I was so grateful to hear that later. Even in the shadow of death, God was with us.

The next day Annie was moved to the Pediatric Intensive Care Unit, or PICU. It was there a doctor told us that she needed "some help" to breathe. They thought it best for us to wait in the hallway while they placed a ventilator in her. Many decisions were made that morning, and I suppose the doctors explained to us what was happening; however, I don't remember much of it. The dark tunnel in my mind allowed bits and pieces of information to filter through, but my focus was on Annie.

I do remember that later that day, a slightly disheveled man, casually dressed in a polo shirt, khakis, and tennis shoes appeared at Annie's door.

"Hi, I'm Dr. Scott, a neurologist here at the hospital. My son is in the room next door. He had an asthma attack today." He looked beyond me to Annie, who was lying motionless behind me. "I'm sorry to hear about your daughter."

"Oh, wow—I'm so sorry to hear about your son. How are *you?* You must be so worried," I said, relieved to shift the attention off our crisis and onto his.

Why was I so quick to redirect the attention onto his problems when all hell was breaking loose on us? I could have told him, "Yes, my daughter. I understand her brain blew up this morning, but they haven't said why yet. I'm thinking it might have something to do with the three other times we brought her down here last year. But no one has confirmed that." Which is what I was thinking. Instead, I smiled, and thanked him for his concern.

Our kids arrived at the hospital—although I don't remember how they got there or who brought them. Two at a time, they sat by Annie's bed and stared at the wires, tubes, and respirator taped to her mouth, overwhelmed by every life-supporting device. Their eyes were rimmed with tears, their faces guarded. All appeared afraid to ask the one question we all wondered, *Is Annie going to live through this?*

"Mom, is Annie going to be okay?" Olivia finally asked.

"I don't know."

"When is she going to wake up?"

"Honey, I don't know."

The PICU waiting room filled up with our friends, family and big coolers packed with food. The first day, Sunday, people cycled in and out of the waiting room. There was a hopeful atmosphere there, with visiting, eating, and praying round the clock. Prayer meetings were scheduled at the church; prayer chains launched all over the country. God heard from a lot of people that Annie was desperately sick and needed more help than the doctors could provide. She needed supernatural healing, just like her daddy did a few years before. That's where our hope was, and that's what we were praying. Annie's brain was injured, and she needed God's healing touch. The elephant silently sitting in the corner of the waiting room, though, was that she might not be healed, she might die.

Monday night, Bill and I switched places. I drove home to be with the other kids and do some laundry while Bill stayed in the ICU room with

Annie. When I got home, I saw that my kids were barely holding it together from the trauma of the morning before.

Olivia's attending to her sister saved Annie's life. Olivia is overwhelmed with emotion and doesn't want to come back home to her bedroom. But I pray that God would impress upon her that she saved Annie's life. She's been at our friend Patti's house last night and now again, tonight. Yet, even if Annie doesn't get any better, even if Annie goes to heaven, I want Olivia to know that before Annie was born, 'Your eyes saw her substance, being yet unformed. And in Your book they all were written, the days fashioned for Annie when as yet there were none of them.' Ps. 139:15-16. Annie's and our days are numbered by You. We love You and we know that You love us. And this life is not all there is—everlasting or eternal life is beyond our comprehension. But we trust You. God, please surround Olivia and Taylor, Peter, Andy, David, Jack and Annie with Your Spirit's comfort and power and grace. Give us all grace to trust You through this time of uncertainty, no matter the outcome. Because the outcome for Annie will be that same destination, whether she gets there before us or after us. Journal, January 22, 2007

Chapter 25:

COMA

Annie's room quickly filled up with cards, a massive pink, butcher-paper get-well poster from her class at church, and mountains of fluffy, stuffed animals. I put our family picture on the counter beside the sink to show the hospital staff that Annie had big brothers and a big sister waiting for her to come home. I often shared the story of Bill's healing with the staff, and how we were praying for Annie's healing. Many of the nurses promised they'd pray too.

Bethany took care of Annie for the first few days in ICU. I wasn't surprised to find out that she was a Christian; her kind, quiet demeanor exuded the love and peace of Jesus. She answered our questions with enough information to maintain hope without promising anything. She stood at the foot of Annie's bed, updating her charts on the computer, and keeping close watch on her vitals flashing on the screens. She adjusted the pillows and turned her from side to side to prevent bed sores, using the soft, stuffed toys as padding around her arms and legs and head. A physical therapist came in and fitted Annie for splints and braces, to prevent her hands or feet from turning inward from spasticity. I was clueless about the ramifications of all these medical procedures; I just wanted Annie to wake up.

On Tuesday, the doctors called a conference to discuss Annie's condition and the results of her initial brain MRI. We crowded into a green conference room: three doctors, a social worker dressed in black, Bill's parents, and us. "Mr. and Mrs. Sullivan, we're afraid we have bad news. Your daughter, Annalee, suffered a severe hypoxic-ischemic brain injury secondary to Addison's Disease. It is a catastrophic brain injury."

Really? I thought. *Don't you think I know she almost died?! Of course, it's a severe brain injury! When I picked her up off the bed Sunday morning, I saw her legs dangling. I saw her blue face. I saw her staring eyes. Don't you think I know this is catastrophic?*

"She may not be able to see or hear ... or walk," they continued.

The color drained from Bill's face. Unfortunately, what the doctors were saying *was* news to him. He thought that when the paramedics showed up at our house and took her to the hospital and she survived, that everything would be fine. The posturing of her body, the pinpoint pupils, the blue color of her skin meant nothing to him. The doctors' assessment was a crushing blow.

Annie's primary diagnosis was Addison's Disease, a type of adrenal insufficiency. Her adrenal glands didn't work, meaning her body had no natural ability to fight illness or respond to physical or emotional stress. Finally, we had an explanation as to why she crashed every time she got any sort of infection. Not enough, or too little, adrenal function when a person is sick causes a domino effect of low blood sugar, low blood pressure, seizures, coma and death. This cascade of events is what happened to Annie. The brain injury was caused by the adrenal crisis she suffered while she was in bed that night. The medics at our house early that morning rescued her right at the point between coma and death. And now Annie remained in that coma.

Looking back, we realized that the first signs of Addison's began when she was 2 years old. Over the course of about a year, she displayed the classic signs of adrenal insufficiency:

1. A golden tan, with darker skin along the creases of the joints of her fingers and toes.

2. Salt craving. Annie loved goldfish crackers, pizza, and ate pepperoni right out of the bag.

3. Exhaustion. She took three-hour naps.

4. Stomach pain and vomiting with multiple episodes prompting visits to the doctor and ER.

5. Emotional symptoms of growing fearfulness, crying, and what was likely depression.

There in the conference room I told the doctors, "I know Annie's injury is catastrophic, but God healed Bill from a terminal illness and He can heal Annie." They looked at me like I was living in an alternate universe. *"Ah, yes, here's another mother wrapped in a blanket of denial. But she'll eventually come around,"* they probably thought.

And you can check your pessimistic attitudes at the door when you go in to examine her too, I thought to myself.

Each day, a team of doctors made their rounds into Annie's room, and each day, their faces grew more somber. *They're human,* I thought. *They're erecting walls around themselves, so our tragedy doesn't inadvertently become theirs.* During morning rounds, they'd report on Annie's status, which wasn't changing. She was in a deep coma and wouldn't rouse when the neurologists called her name, or when they would touch her skin with pinpricks. The longer she was unresponsive, the more pessimistic the prognosis became. I understood their dilemma. They wanted to make sure we understood the stakes. But that was my daughter lying there, and I needed someone to give me a shred of hope. *What does it hurt to give a parent a minuscule reason to hope?* I thought. I'm all about telling the truth, but *how about a little hope to balance out the dump trucks of truth you keep unloading in here?*

Later that week, I went down to the cafeteria to take a break while Bill sat beside Annie's bed, watching her motionless body. After I left, Bill noticed her eyebrow twitch as if she were about to open it.

"Look!" he said to the nurse, "Look at her eyebrow!" He jumped up and stood by the bed, waiting for the nurse to confirm the good news. The nurse watched Annie for a moment, and then a dark shadow swept across her face. She hit the call button and a team of doctors rushed in. Annie wasn't waking up as Bill had hoped. No, her eye twitch signaled breakthrough seizure activity. The doctors loaded her up with more sedatives, which made the twitches go away. Bill slumped back down on the foldout couch, his head in his hands. "Even good news is bad news," he told me later.

Each time the doctors came in to discuss how dire Annie's condition was, the social worker dressed in black appeared in the hallway outside the door. Bill noted that she bore a strong resemblance to the Angel of Death. When Annie took a turn for the worse, there stood the social worker, all dressed in black, almost levitating above the floor. I'm sure she was just trying to do her job; be a support to the parents of a child dangling between life and death. God provided support, however, through our friends both inside and outside of the hospital. They came around with small (and sometimes big) acts of kindness and words of encouragement to lighten our emotional load. One of my friends from church worked in the hospital's rehab department and stopped by one day with a few water bottles for us. I knew she had experience with brain-injured patients, and I wanted to know, did *she* think Annie would get better?

"What is God telling you?" I asked her.

"Hope," was all she said. There. She said it. *Hope.* She didn't give us any promises, but she didn't take away our hope, either.

Another friend from our church, Pam, worked downstairs in Dialysis and brought me lattes every morning before she started her day. Short, with cropped gray hair, no-nonsense Pam had a soft spot in her heart for Annie that began from the time she first rocked her in the nursery at our church. I was thankful Pam worked in the same hospital that would become Annie's second home.

My friend, Kim, who organized our yard cleanup when Bill was sick and brought us that *Happy Healing* cake years before, took time away from her job at the local trauma hospital to sit with me for four days straight. Nancy, another friend from church who also volunteered to clean our house, came by with a blue comforter for Bill and me to use when we took turns staying at the hospital. She gave it to me with tears in her eyes saying, "I needed to give this blanket to you. I just wanted it to give you a big *hug.*"

Even the scheduled nurses who worked with Annie were, for the most part, incredibly encouraging. One fussed with Annie's long, blond hair that had become a mass of tangles from lying in the hospital bed, and as she leaned in close, she cupped Annie's face in her hands. "I have a good feeling about this kid. I don't always know how it's going to turn out, but I have a good feeling about this one." And then a young female resident pulled me aside in Annie's room after a particularly depressing discussion with the doctors about Annie's newest MRI. "Don't be discouraged," she said. "Two kids can have the same awful MRI and have two very different outcomes. Don't lose hope." Hope. That's all I needed to make it through one more day.

Most nights I spent in the parents' sleeping rooms on the fifth floor. Sleep, however, was constantly interrupted by the traumatic vision replaying in my mind of what happened to Annie.

Why can't I sleep? My mind rehearses the events of Sunday morning: finding Annie, calling the ambulance, ER, then now. The little body downstairs is Annie's shell. Annie is gone from us. Lord, even now I know You can heal her. I believe that. But do You want to heal her? Are You going to heal her? Our hearts are broken—Bill's, Taylor's, Peter's, David's, Jack's, Olivia's and mine. Our hearts are so broken. Lord, we need You to undertake for us. 'The eternal God is your refuge, and underneath are the everlasting arms.' Deuteronomy 33:27. God, we need You now. Journal, January 24, 2007.

Chapter 26:

WAKING?

Typically, people don't wake up from comas like they do in the movies; one minute they're asleep, the next they're looking around wondering what happened. More often it's a painstaking snail's pace from no response to tiny glimmers of hope. That was the case with Annie.

Three days after Annie's brain injury, I sat beside her bed listening to the whoosh, whoosh of the ventilator when she suddenly started making movements with her lips. "Look," I said to Bethany. "She's moving her mouth!" Bethany's eyes grew wide and she came closer to the bed to watch.

"Annie," she said, "Annie, can you move your legs?"

Both of her legs moved almost imperceptibly. She swallowed and coughed a little over her ventilator. The neurologist came in and said Annie's reflexes in her pupils were good, too, all of which was incredibly encouraging.

The next day, Vickie came in to read to Annie. She brought *The Napping House,* the book they'd shared together so many times when Bill and I were in Ireland. The irony was Annie seemed to be napping now, and nothing seemed to rouse her that day. That is, until she heard Vickie's voice.

"Hi Annie, it's me, Miss Vickie," she said, sitting down in the rocker close to the head of the hospital bed.

"I brought your favorite story. Would you like me to read it to you?"

Annie lay still, her blond braids laid out flat on the pillow behind her head. Vickie began reading. The nurse left the room to check on something but returned and looked up at Annie's heart monitor, her eyes growing wide. "What are you doing?" she asked Vickie. It was more of a rhetorical question; she could see Vickie was reading to her.

"I'm reading to Annie," Vickie said.

"Look, her heart rate is up!" the nurse said pointing at the monitor, "and that's a *good* thing."

Annie recognized Miss Vickie's soothing voice and the story they'd read together so many times before. Her heart rate showed what her little body could not—that she could *hear* and that she was still *in there*. Annie could hear! No doctor had officially confirmed it yet, but the evidence was clear to everyone in the room that day.

I thought back to years before, lying in a recovery room right after the birth of our second-born, Peter. His was an emergency C-section delivery; the umbilical cord had prolapsed, cutting off his oxygen supply, risking his life and mine. We were whisked from a labor room into an operating room, where an anesthesiologist gently and efficiently knocked me out so the doctor could deliver Peter in record time. About a half hour later I was in the recovery room eavesdropping on the nurses who were talking about me. They thought I was asleep, but I was listening to everything they said.

"Is Mrs. Sullivan awake, yet?"

"No, she's still asleep. Should be waking up soon, though."

I'm awake! I can hear everything you're saying! I can't move a bone in my body, but I hear everything you're saying about me, I thought to myself. What an odd feeling, being perfectly lucid, hearing everything, yet not being able to communicate to the nurses. I'll never forget it.

So, I knew Annie was in there and could hear us. While Vickie was sitting across the bed from me, I saw a shadow of a facial expression flicker across Annie's face, then barely perceptible movements of her mouth and tongue. She was trying, I could tell she was trying *so hard* to let us know she was in there.

Because we now knew Annie could hear, we put an iPod dock on the shelf next to the head of her hospital bed and played classical music, instrumental hymns, and her favorite: Vince Guaraldi's *A Charlie Brown Christmas* music. We wanted to use every means we could to coax her out of her coma. And the soft music was a comfort to Bill and me too.

Our kids continued to come and go, visiting Annie when their school or work schedules allowed. Olivia came in one evening and decided to paint Annie's fingernails. Since Annie wasn't moving much, there was plenty of time for her nails to dry. Later that week, Peter came in to visit after work and I noticed he had a new tattoo on his neck. I turned his chin so I could get a better look, and there in flowing script was his little sister's name, *Annalee*. Everyone has their own way of dealing with crisis. Peter's was to wear his broken heart for his little sister on his neck.

Five days after Annie's brain injury, a decision was made that she should have a trial wean off the ventilator. She was still in a coma-like state, and in the back of my mind I knew if she couldn't breathe on her own, eventually other "decisions" would be made. We knew all about mechanical ventilation from when Bill was sick and having trouble breathing. Back then, Bill decided he wasn't going to go the ventilator route but just say goodbye and go to heaven when he could no longer breathe by himself. Given similar circumstances we'd make the same decision for Annie, although I don't remember specifically talking about it with Bill in that first week. Our values were clear. We valued life, but we weren't afraid of death.

Okay, that's a lie. I was terrified Annie might die during the vent wean. I was beyond anxious. I didn't want to be there and watch, but I didn't want to leave her alone either, because I was afraid she might die. Now the fact is, if she couldn't breathe by herself, the vent could be put in again right away. But I guess I didn't put that all together in my mind that day. It happened to be my mother's birthday, January 26th. The irony that Annie, named after my mother, might die on her grandmother's birthday wasn't lost on me. So, I braced myself for it. In my mind, the two options for Annie were complete healing or death. A third option—permanent, severe disability, hadn't yet crossed my mind.

The respiratory therapist breezed in that day with a confident air like she could do ventilator weans in her sleep, maybe even with one arm tied behind her back. We both knew, however, what was going on: Annie needed to prove she could breathe on her own. The therapist gloved up outside Annie's room, came in and put a tray of suction equipment on the table beside the bed. She carefully took the tape from Annie's cheeks that secured the ventilator and slipped the tube out of her mouth. Immediately she began suctioning Annie's mouth and throat so she wouldn't choke on her secretions. The suctioning caused Annie to cough, "a good sign," the nurse noted. My hands gripped the bedrail as I whispered desperate prayers, not taking my eyes off Annie. She was so weak, her neck didn't support the weight of her head, and it wobbled from side to side without support of rolled up towels. After about four hours, her oxygen level was 97% and CO_2 was 35—which was higher than the normal range of 23-29.

"We'll keep an eye on that," the nurse said, "and hopefully she'll improve quickly. But she's breathing on her own."

"And she's alive," I whispered under my breath.

The devastation to Annie is almost more than I can bear. She's got no muscle tone in her arms or neck or back...she as limp as a dishrag. Lord, please heal her quickly or mercifully take her home with You. Lord, You are able to heal her, but

I don't know if You want to. Why would You want to? I don't know. God—my heart is broken. Please heal her. Journal, January 25, 2007

By February 5th, Annie was stable enough to be moved out of ICU and into an endocrine unit on the second floor. The staff at our church signed the back of a big wooden sign and brought it to the hospital to put in Annie's room. It belonged to Amanda, the 16-year-old daughter of one of Bill's co-workers, Carrie. Amanda was born with multiple disabilities, but a lack of faith was not one of them. After Annie went into the hospital, Amanda took the sign off her bedroom wall, gave it to her mother and said, "I want to give this to Annie." The sign said, *"With God all things are possible."* I put it on a shelf above Annie's hospital bed, so all who entered would know exactly Who it was that we were putting our faith in.

Chapter 27:

A IS FOR AGITATION

Our children did their best to hold themselves together at home. They were old enough to be alone, do their laundry, and answer the door when friends brought over meals. Nonetheless, between seeing paramedics work on Annie in our living room, and hospital visits to see their comatose little sister, my kids all suffered significant trauma and needed the comfort of a familiar adult to be with them. Bill was juggling work and hospital visits, and I was juggling Annie and doctors. Enter my sister Rebecca who flew out from Oklahoma to serve as surrogate housemother for a month. Rebecca talks like me, laughs like me and looks like me, so the kids hardly knew I was gone. Their only hint was that Rebecca and I diverge in the area of laundry. She loves to do laundry; I don't, and delegated laundry to my kids by the time they were 10. Rebecca, however, works out her anxieties by doing laundry. All of it, all the time. When our laundry was done, she moved on to organizing the entire house, room by room. Rebecca's handle on our home enabled me to focus on Annie, and the brain injury agitation that was overtaking her little body.

Agitation, or *neurostorming* is common after a severe brain injury. Most believe the storming to be caused by the brain reorganizing itself. Annie's agitation started six days after her brain injury.

Agitation refers to extreme behavior, including restlessness, big mood swings, aggressiveness, and taking action without thinking about what one is doing first. Agitation can begin during the early stages of brain injury recovery, when an individual is not fully conscious or when cognition (thinking skills) is impaired. Past researchers have suspected that agitation may interfere with the rehabilitation process and result in less than desired outcomes for recovery. Individuals with traumatic brain injury and agitation are more likely to be discharged to facilities that can provide constant supervision than to home. Research about agitation has been limited.[24]

By early February Annie was into her second week of screaming, thrashing, and general mayhem. She rubbed her little toes raw from banging them on the sides of her hospital bed until the nurses put heavy vinyl pads on the rails to protect her skin. A netted tent was brought in to cover her bed so she wouldn't fall out. (I was deathly afraid of her climbing out and falling onto the floor, however, after her brain injury Annie quit using her hands in any meaningful way. Sad for her recovery, but safe for staying in bed.) About the only thing that calmed her down were sedatives and cuddle time rocking on Mommy's or Daddy's lap. But sometimes even that didn't help. Annie's anxiety and confusion often eclipsed our best efforts, and she'd simply thrash around as we held her. When we needed a break, faithful friends would come and sit with Annie. One of my friends confided that after getting off the elevator, she knew the way to Annie's room by following the noise.

This time was particularly trying for both Bill and me. We met the challenges by taking quiet moments to assess each other's feelings and grieve over what had happened to Annie, praying constantly for ourselves, for our

---

24   http://www.biausa.org/tbims-abstracts/
       the-influence-of-agitation-onrecovery-from-traumatic-brain-injury.

other children, and for Annie. We felt the prayers of many people holding us up too. However, we both had what would be described as anxiety attacks on the way down to the hospital when it was our turn to stay with her. I'd pull into the hospital driveway, and the vague knot in the pit of my stomach clamped down with a vengeance. More than once I thought it wouldn't be an unreasonable request to ask the nurses to share some of Annie's sedatives with me.

I needed to know how long this craziness was going to last, so another friend from our church, a nurse practitioner of neurosurgery at the local trauma hospital, came in to look at Annie and give me her impressions. In her experience with adults, patients don't know who they are, where they are, and often their eyes "rove" like Annie's did. She assured me that after all that, it's not uncommon for patients to come out the other side with their personalities intact. I wondered if Annie was going to be anywhere near intact when she came out on the other side.

Lord—please relieve (Annie's) anxiety and frustration and coughing. Please, please, please Lord—hear my prayer and the prayers of so many other saints around the country and around the world. Lord—please heal Annie's eyes, memory, arms, legs—all of her. ...And I do ask again, Lord, Annie would be another miracle of healing. Please God, hear our prayers. Journal, February 5, 2007

Back to square one with the agitation. I need to go get some coffee to have enough energy to deal with this kiddo. Lord—connect Annie's dots in her brain— strengthen her upper body, neck and arms and please heal her completely. She has a hearing test scheduled for 1 p.m. today. I know she can hear. Praise God. Journal, February 13, 2007

At some point, the doctors tested her hearing to see if it had been spared. And of course, the audiology test showed she could hear perfectly. I figured that had been established when her heart rate went up when Vickie read to her three weeks before. That was one part of her brain that mercifully remained intact. In fact, Annie seemed to be coming out more and more each day, like a turtle peeking its head out of its shell. Occasionally we'd see shadows of her former facial expressions, too. Not smiles, necessarily, but expressions around her eyes. We don't realize how much communication, how much of *who we are*, is written on our faces, until it is gone. This happened when Bill was sick. He became flat and vacant. Knowing what he was thinking or how he was feeling was hard to discern, and only revealed by asking specific questions. As Annie emerged from her coma, terror often appeared in her eyes that roved the room, scanning for invisible threats known only to her. Terror slowly, almost imperceptibly, was replaced with fleeting shades of old, familiar, Annie-type expressions. Vanishing almost as soon as they appeared, they were visible long enough to give me hope that my sweet Annie was still inside.

Because she could no longer chew and swallow food, Annie was fed through a nasogastric (NG) tube, and her thrashing inevitably dislodged this thin, yellow tube leading from her food bag to her nose and into her gut. The NG tube regularly would go flying, spraying sickeningly sweet, vanilla formula all over everything within a four-foot radius. Replacing the NG tube was traumatic for Annie. The nurses tightly swaddled her in a big blanket and then gently—or not so gently, depending on how cooperative Annie was, would jam it back into her nose and down her throat. This process occurred fourteen times while she was in the hospital.

Although the auditory test showed perfect hearing, Annie's vision was still a question, and her speech so far was zero. Coughing, screaming, and crying were the only noises coming from her lips. And although her hearing test was a victory, by the middle of the month the agitation was taking a toll on all of us, and I was feeling as unhinged as Annie.

Another day in the salt mine. Annie seems to be more "in there" and coming more "out here"—but I'm still concerned about her sight and speech. Lord—please restore both to her please. This is the third, going into fourth week here. Seems like our life before was someone else's—a dream. I am suffering a little (a lot) from post-traumatic stress syndrome. Anytime Annie throws up (this morning at 4 am) or goes into orbit because the nurses are doing something (this evening at 8 p.m.) I just about h...Okay—just as I wrote that SHE THREW UP!! I—Lord help me!! God, when is this hyper alert going to end? I think my adrenal glands are going to burst. God, I need You to calm me down. I am out of peace, out of energy, and I can't stand to see Annie living in the shadow of death. It is totally freaking me out. Journal, February 14, 2007

Bill and I tag-teamed back and forth from the house to the hospital. He'd stay at the hospital on the weekends to give me time off to regroup at home, and I stayed at the hospital during the week so he could work. We already had weathered many crises in our marriage, but this one topped them all by far. I read somewhere that one of the ways to keep your marriage from completely falling apart during a crisis is to find time to be alone with one another. Being intimate provides us with comfort and healing from grief or loss, the article said. Realistically, sex was the last thing on either my mind or Bill's. Okay, at least mine. We were shell-shocked with Annie's brain injury, coma, agitation, and the exhaustion from being at the hospital for what had been a month by then. Exhaustion from dealing with the grief of our other six kids. Exhaustion from adjusting to a new normal that didn't include much of our former way of life.

Yet February, as well as being the national month of brain injury agitation and storming, was the month of love. Valentine's Day. Some well-meaning friends got us a gift card to a restaurant near the hospital, so Bill and I got dressed up, our friend came to sit with Annie at the hospital, and we drove to the restaurant. We walked in, sat down, and looked around at all the other couples enjoying their normal lives, cozily sharing secrets in the candlelight. I felt a bit guilty for leaving Annie and indulging in a dinner alone with Bill, but I also knew we needed to continue being "we" in order to get through this crisis. Tonight was an opportunity to drive a stake in the ground that we were not going to drift apart.

I stabbed the chicken on my salad with my fork. "We've got two hours until we have to be back at the hospital."

"Well, we can relax. Two hours is plenty of time for a nice dinner."

"I had a little more in mind," I said. "There's a room at that hotel across the street from the hospital with our name on it."

He raised his eyebrow and a smile crept onto the corners of his mouth. "Hmm."

Our little tryst that night was a reminder we would continue to walk through this hell we were in—together.

Back at the hospital, on good days when she wasn't yelling, we worked with Annie to try to help her relearn the use of her hands. Denise, a nurse and the wife of our pastor, along with our 18-year-old son, Andy, came down to the hospital to help Annie drum on a book. Annie sat on Andy's lap while he held her hands to drum. After a few tries, Annie initiated drumming herself. Andy played drums in the high school band and for the youth group at our church. He was in his second semester of college, which he eventually had to repeat after Annie's brain injury wrecked his grades. Somehow teaching his little sister to reuse her hands and arms seemed more important than studying.

Annie's next hurdle was to learn how to sit in a wheelchair. Bill decided to help Annie practice sitting one evening but practicing sitting in her wheelchair was something she hated. Bill dutifully lifted her into the wheelchair for twenty calm minutes followed by ten grumpy ones. Protest she did. Loudly.

It always seemed that a block to her progress was the boatload of sedating medicine she was on, some medicines to control seizures and some to control her agitation. And some so the kid in the next room could sleep at night. I knew the drugs were slowing Annie's thinking, and I thought if we could just wean her off all her medicine, she'd be more alert and be more herself. What a stupid naive idea, in retrospect. One day we tried delaying her regularly scheduled Valium at 2:00 p.m. An hour later, Annie was climbing the walls with yelling, thrashing her arms and legs, and yelling. Did I mention she was yelling? The pharmacy couldn't send the Valium fast enough. The nurse gave Annie some around 3:30 p.m. and then we gave her another smaller dose at 4:30 p.m. By 6 p.m. she was still going nuts, biting herself and thrashing around, so we gave her Benadryl. At 6:45 p.m. she was still agitated, so I got a nurse to sit with her so I could get some dinner. As if I could eat.

I walked out into the hallway, up the elevator and into the cafeteria, wandered around, bought a bottle of water because they were out of prosecco, and then went outside to call Denise. She prayed with me and gave me some ideas on easier, more gradual ways to wean off the Valium. I walked back down to Annie's room and there she was in bed, sound asleep with the nurse's aide sitting beside her in the rocking chair. "Thank you, Jesus, thank you, thank you, thank you," I whispered.

The nurse's aide looked familiar, and I recognized her from the time Annie had been hospitalized a year before when she had first adrenal crisis, but before she was diagnosed with Addison's. Annie was in the hospital at that time for three days, but she revived after receiving IV fluids and was discharged, without tests for, or a diagnosis of, adrenal insufficiency. The nurse's aide interrupted my thoughts and asked, "Annie wasn't like this before, was she?"

"No. No, she wasn't," I blurted out. Annie was normal before. Perfect. Laughing, singing, walking, talking, eating, cuddling her Raggedy Ann doll. But not now.

Why, God? Why, why, why? I cried to myself that night. *Why didn't the doctors figure this out the three other times she was here last year? Why are You doing this to Annie? Why did You let this happen? Why didn't I research her symptoms on the internet and figure it out myself? Why didn't she have a seizure during the day when I could have helped her immediately? I don't understand this at all and I'm sick of putting a positive spin on this, as if that's even possible. God, what are You doing? Could You please just tell us so we could know too? Don't rob Annie's personality and health away from her. Weren't we already here a few years ago? Didn't we already go through this when Bill was sick? Why do You keep allowing these things to happen?* Journal, February 19, 2007

Later that night Bill's brother, Kevin, called me on Annie's hospital room phone from his home in California. Wrong night for him; he got a major earful from me. Everything I'd just dumped on God, I dumped on Kevin.

"I'll be up on the next plane if you need me there," he said as his voice caught.

I felt guilty for his sadness. He couldn't fix this. He couldn't fix Annie. "No, your prayers are the best thing you can do for us, Kevin."

And I knew that.

Lord, please help me to trust You, I whispered as I hung up.

On good days when Annie wasn't too agitated, I'd hold her in my lap on the glider rocker and read to her. One of her favorite books from before her brain injury was a large, pink Disney Princess picture book. I read it to her there in her hospital room, and the familiar words seemed to settle her down. Belle, Snow White, Cinderella…Annie followed the action on the pages from left to right with her eyes. I knew then that she could see. The doctors hadn't pronounced her able to see, but I knew she could see. When I told the doctors that she could see, they didn't believe me. It wasn't until a few months later when an ophthalmologist who practiced outside the hospital confirmed it that they believed it.

Toward the end of February, we were out of ideas to calm Annie's agitation until a nurse named Jenny said, "Let's try the big bathtub." For over a month, I'd only given Annie sponge baths, and the thought of trying to lift her thrashing arms and legs into a regular bathtub was unnerving.

"Bring your swimming suit from home, put it on, and get in there with her," Jenny instructed me. *Oh, wonderful,* I thought. So not only was I worried about Annie getting in the tub, I also now got to show my love for her by bringing my cellulite to the party.

"That way, you can hold her—she'll love it," Jenny assured me.

"Hmm." I felt my blood pressure going up but obediently put on my swimsuit, and with my friend Jan's, and nurse Jenny's help, we wheeled Annie into the big bathtub room which was down the hall and around the corner from her hospital room. We filled the tub with very warm water, and I got in. Then Jenny and Jan lifted Annie and carefully slid her into the water and onto my lap. The water was deep, almost to Annie's chin, but as soon as she felt the warm water around her, she completely relaxed into my arms. Peace washed across her face, and for the first time in a month her body felt completely at ease, all tension melted away. When Jenny washed her hair, Annie started to protest, showing new strength in her neck and upper body, so even her resisting was a great encouragement for all of us. While I rocked her later that evening in her hospital room, I longed to hold her and look up at the stars in the night sky again.

Lord, please heal Annie completely: speech, sight, memory, hearing, strength. Lord, please heal her. What about tonight? Could You heal her tonight while she slept? Then we would have a HUGE party and sing and shout and celebrate what God did. Wouldn't that be so cool? Lord, if it is within the realm of Your will...Lord, if You are willing, please heal Annie's brain and body tonight while she sleeps just like You healed her daddy seven years ago. I know You are able. I pray You are willing, Lord. Please. Journal, February 22, 2007

The next day Annie had her best day yet: alert, sitting up tall, trying so hard to make her arms and legs do what she wanted them to do. Peter came in during lunch and told her to use her "angry eyes," a trick she used to do for her older brothers and sister after seeing Mr. Potato Head do it in the movie *Toy Story*. She promptly scowled at Peter. Then he asked her to smile, and she bared her teeth. This was a remarkable leap, because responding to commands is a big deal in brain injury progress. Up to that point, Annie hadn't responded to much of anything.

Kristi, another friend from church and a pediatric speech therapist, sat with Annie so I could get some dinner in the cafeteria one day. She sang, *If You're Happy and You Know It,* while helping Annie to clap her hands and stomp her feet. Annie tried to clap her hands and she moved her feet when Kristi cued her. After Kristi finished working with her, Annie was the calmest and most alert she'd been in a month. It was so encouraging to see God knitting her brain back together little by little.

By the end of February, the hospital staff discussed discharging Annie to our home, but a few things needed to happen first. Annie refused to eat orally and was still being fed through the NG tube. Whether the fourteen NG changes made her reluctant to eat or whether she refused food because of sensory damage to her brain, she threw up a lot. Brushing her teeth with a spec of toothpaste on the toothbrush was my first introduction to her oral sensory aversion. As soon as the toothpaste touched her tongue, she turned inside out. The NG tube went flying, and her stomach contents covered her wheelchair. From that day on, when I took out the toothbrush, she'd give me the side eye of suspicion. Occupational therapists who tried to get her to eat got the same response. Pudding, applesauce, tiny spoons of apple juice, any of it made Annie's sensory system go on tilt, and the NG tube would come out, along with whatever was inside her gut. To eliminate the problems with NG tubes flying out of Annie's nose, and the pain she endured when reinserting them, the doctors thought it best to place a G-tube into her stomach. A G-tube, or gastrostomy tube, would go straight into Annie's stomach so she could get the nutrition she needed without having to physically eat. It was another sign of defeat for me—I wanted her to relearn to eat—but a G-tube would make the process of feeding her doable until then.

On March 1st Annie had her gastrostomy tube surgery, as well as her second brain MRI and her hearing test. Her hearing test revealed perfect hearing in both ears—thank you, Lord. The surgeon came out after her G-tube surgery to say it went well, with the exception that she held her breath when they made the incision. I don't know why the surgeon shared that information with us. He said that they gave her more sedation after that and then she breathed again. He turned and walked back into the surgery area, and Bill and I sat down, stunned at the information we'd just heard.

Finally, a nurse came out and said one of us could go back into the recovery room. Bill deferred to me, so I went in and found Annie in a crib-like hospital bed looking pale and clammy. I know now that was a sign that she needed more hydrocortisone to recover from her surgery, however I can't remember if she got any then or not. In any event, I sat down on a stool beside her crib and Annie immediately threw up blood. Already on hyper-alert for a month, I lost it and started shaking while trying to clean up Annie. The nurses quickly came over to help me as they explained that the blood was residual fluids from the surgery. *Whatever,* I thought. This suffering and misery Annie was enduring was sending me into orbit. Later, Bill told me to take a break and go home, and he stayed with her in the hospital that night, which was good because I was emotionally fried and had to consciously force myself to calm down every time Annie had one of these crises...which was way too often.

After that surgery, Annie never used her angry eyes again. She never again clapped her hands or stomped her feet. I wondered how long her breathing had stopped in surgery; it wasn't like she had brain cells to spare.

Jan, who had helped with Annie's bath, came to the hospital a few days later. She and her husband, Erik, had a son with a congenital heart defect requiring multiple hospitalizations. They knew all about health crises. She assessed my mental state and decided it was time for a pep talk. We walked down to the empty cafeteria and sat down at a table. I picked at the tater tots on my tray while she lovingly let me have it.

"Jean, you've got to put on your big girl panties and suck it up."

"I know I'm a mess." I looked at her and wanted to believe I could do it. I seriously doubted I could care for a little girl who was so medically fragile. The thought of taking Annie home was terrifying to me.

"You need to trust God. He's going to help you. But you need to trust Him."

"Yeah, I know."

"You can do this. You *have* to do this. But you've got to get a grip."

Chapter 28:

LEARNING CURVE

The first month after Annie's brain injury, I was suffering from some degree of post-traumatic stress disorder. When falling to sleep, the images of her blue, limp body lying on the living room floor played over and over in my mind. In the morning all I thought was, *is she going to live through this?* My next thought was *Am I going to live through this?* Now, if that's the condition my semi-rational adult mind was in, what anxiety did my other children feel?

Each of our kids' perspectives about Annie's brain injury was influenced by their age, their personality, their fears about how this would affect them, and their concerns about what this meant to us as a family. Another part of the equation was their ability to absorb the added burden to themselves, whatever that meant to them individually. Some kids are more resilient than others. Each of our children responded differently to the trauma of losing the little sister they once knew.

I read somewhere that brain injury never affects just one person in a family, but rather it is like a bomb that goes off. Not only is the patient affected, but the whole family reels. This was our experience. After watching their sister almost die, along with the daily grief of the loss of the 'old' Annie, how could their own emotional collateral damage be avoided? Bill and I asked each of them more than once if they'd like to go to counseling. All of them assured us that they were 'fine.' Well, they weren't fine. That is a deep regret of mine, that I didn't insist on some form of counseling for them sooner rather than later.

Annie was initially in the hospital for 52 days. And in that 52 days, Taylor and Peter, adults by then, came and went to the hospital as often as their work allowed. But for the younger ones, her hospital stay happened during the school year, during David's basketball season, and during Andy's second semester of college. Many of their activities either ground to a halt or got only half the attention they needed. Andy spent a lot of time at the hospital those first few weeks, and as a result, flunked out of that college semester. (But eventually did graduate!) Olivia, in middle school, and Jack and David, in high school, were physically at school, but their minds were at the hospital with Annie. Fortunately, they all got a pass from their teachers. If they showed up to class, they got an A. If they missed class, they got an A. I really don't think there was any way they could fail. Their teachers and school counselors, rock stars, all of them, continually checked on them, encouraged them, supported them. Every one of the teachers and school counselors who tended to my emotionally trashed kids deserve medals. They may have missed some learning that year that would have granted them scholarships to University X, Y, or Z. Oh well. They were learning bigger lessons, like the preciousness and brevity of life, the inherent value of those with physical and intellectual disabilities, and the faithfulness of God in the midst of crushing loss.

These lessons were learned over time, slowly, ploddingly, painfully. Bill and I were keenly aware we needed to focus not only on Annie, but *all* our children. We intentionally used routine errands to listen to them vent, allowing them to be free with their feelings and talk openly about how they felt, anger and all. The only line we drew was that angry words were not acceptable in front of Annie because we always made the assumption she could understand what was being said. We prayed with them, cried with them, and assured them God loved them, loved our family, and loved Annie. No, we didn't know why He allowed this to happen. No, we didn't know how it was all going to work out; however, we constantly assured them of our love for them and God's love for us.

As we prepared to leave the hospital, not only were we shedding the security blanket of 24/7 medical care for Annie, but we also were putting on a new role as parents of a child with severe disabilities. Our learning curve was steep. Annie had complex medical needs, not only relating to her brain injury, but also from the underlying cause of the brain injury: primary adrenal insufficiency, or Addison's Disease. People with adrenal insufficiency require daily cortisol supplementation, usually in the form of hydrocortisone tablets, given throughout the day to mimic the normal circadian rhythm of cortisol production. The adrenal glands secrete cortisol beginning around 3 a.m., peaking first thing in the morning then slowly declining until bedtime.

When Annie was discharged, we knew very little about Addison's and how to manage it. It is a relatively rare disease, and the only other people I'd heard of with Addison's were President John F. Kennedy and the Australian singer, Helen Reddy.

The doctors gave us their best guess as to the dose of hydrocortisone Annie needed for her size and weight, and then they sent us home. The first morning she woke up vomiting, a classic sign of low cortisol. However, we didn't know that yet. All we knew was vomiting put her at risk for aspiration because she couldn't yet coordinate her swallowing, breathing and throwing up movements. Terrified she would die in a similar way to how we found her the morning of January 21st, we called 911. Then we called them again the next morning. We ended up calling 911 a few more times, until we figured out the reason she kept throwing up in the morning was because she wasn't getting enough hydrocortisone. In fact, it was quite a while before the doctors understood Annie needed about double the dose of most kids with Addison's.

The way they figured it out was by me telling them, repeatedly, "She needs more hydrocortisone."

It slowly dawned on me there was no other kid like Annie, and the doctors were really shooting in the dark with most of her care. I realized then that *I* was the expert on Annie and needed to learn all I could about her diagnoses, and how they interacted with one another, along with the 15 prescriptions she needed to take. I was completely overwhelmed. At some point, I realized that I could not keep her alive, God needed to do that. But I also needed to quit expecting the doctors to have all the answers regarding her care. Because they simply didn't.

Most people with Addison's Disease just have Addison's Disease. They don't have Addison's *and* a brain injury *and* a seizure disorder *and* central high blood pressure caused by brain injury *and* are G-tube fed *and* lame *and* nonverbal *and* sensory averse to touch. Our friend, Erik, stopped by the hospital one evening and gave me two pieces of advice: *Look at trends, not days* and *you are your child's advocate.* I finally got a clue. The fact was, Annie had a neurologist, a pediatrician, a nephrologist, and an endocrinologist following her. These people had full caseloads themselves, and it was unreasonable to think they spent as much time mulling over her quirky medical problems as we did. So, we provided her doctors with detailed, accurate information we kept on a daily log that Bill designed, and then together came up with a game plan for whatever problem Annie was having. And as parents of a kid with complicated medical issues, Bill and I needed to be Annie's advocates and not just mindlessly do whatever the doctors said.

Our day began between 5:00 and 5:30 a.m. when I got up, went into the kitchen to crush her pills, mix them with a tiny bit of water, draw them up in a syringe, open a can of formula to put into her G-tube bag, go into her room to give her medicine and start her food. Sleeping in was never an option. If she woke up before we did, she'd summon us by sticking her finger down her throat and gagging herself. It was effective. If we were fast, we'd make it into her bedroom before she threw up. If we were slow, we'd have

a mess to clean up. Sometimes her vomiting was simply a need for hydrocortisone, and she actually was nauseated. Other times she just wanted our
attention. Usually we didn't know which was which. Was she gagging herself
because she wanted our attention or because she was about to go into an
adrenal crisis? She couldn't talk, so she couldn't tell us.

To duplicate Annie's natural circadian cortisol rhythm, we gave her
hydrocortisone pills at 6 a.m., 12 noon and 6 p.m. If Annie didn't get the
right dose of hydrocortisone at regular intervals each day, on time, she could
go into an adrenal crisis. When she was sick, we'd give her either double or
triple the regular hydrocortisone dose. This mimicked how the body increases
cortisol production to fight illness. In the event Annie threw up her medicine, we'd need to give her an emergency injection of Solu-Cortef, which is
cortisol in liquid form. We learned that without proper treatment, the time
from adrenal crisis to death can be as little as 30 minutes.

In the morning after giving Annie her medicines, I'd change her diaper, lift her out of the padded hospital bed in her room, and walk her down
the hall to her daddy, who would be waiting to hold her in the living room
recliner. "Walking" meant standing behind her, my hands under her armpits,
and gently prompting her with one of my knees behind her bottom. Her
brain remembered to move her feet to step left and right, but she had no
balance to walk independently. Bill held Annie in a snuggly blanket on his
lap for about an hour each morning while I showered, got dressed and did
some puttering. We'd have a short Bible and prayer time with Annie, and
then he'd go to work.

Bill loved his time with Annie in the morning. Often Annie just went
back to sleep on his lap, laying her head on his chest and resting her hand on
top of her blanket. With her sensory aversion, the only time anyone could
touch her hands was when she was asleep. And when she was asleep, Bill
held her hand.

We soon realized that Annie could never be unsupervised, even in
the next room. When she slept in her bed, a video monitored her from the

time we put her down at night until she woke in the morning. Each night I slept with one ear open, listening to the video monitor on the floor by my bed. If Annie had a seizure, I jumped up to help her. When she had drop seizures in her bed, she'd get tangled up in her feeding tube, which slowly ran with food and water all night, and hurt herself if the tube was pulling out of her stomach.

If Annie had drop seizures while playing on the floor with her toys, she fell forward violently, often ending up on her stomach with her legs out behind her. Because she had sensory aversion in her hands, she didn't use them to right herself. She just flailed about, struggling until someone came to help her. Thankfully our family was large enough that someone always had their eyes on Annie. We took turns sitting with her, watching her pick up toys, mouth them as an infant would, and throw them.

She did have frequent drop seizures, in spite of taking three seizure drugs and having a VNS, (vagus nerve stimulator) placed under her skin. She eventually developed Lennox-Gastaut Syndrome, a particularly difficult type of epilepsy to control. Along with the VNS and seizure medicine, we tried the Ketogenic Diet for about six months to control the seizures. However, we discovered that one of the goals of the Ketogenic Diet is to lower blood sugar, which directly conflicts with the hydrocortisone's effect of raising blood sugar. The competing effects of the diet and hydrocortisone seemed to cause more seizures, so we quit the Ketogenic Diet.

Brain injury is unlike any other physical disability. Our brains hold the essence of who we are: our memory, voice, ideas, and personality. Are we funny or serious? Introvert, extrovert? Organized or random? If the injury to the brain is severe, much of the outward expression of our personalities, and what we do, is lost. With Annie, her physical injuries were catastrophic, but her mental injuries were more so. Her little voice that used to sing songs and recite Bible verses—gone. Waking me with her cheerful, *"It's morning-time!"* —gone. Telling me "It's time *for bref-kiss,"* asking for more marsh-lellow cereal—all gone.

One day I came into the living room while David was on Annie duty. He sat in big stuffed leather chair watching her pick up toys, mouth them, and throw them. This wasn't the little sister who played Slug Bug with him a few months before, the little *Cinderella-la* twirling in the pink tiara and sparkly tulle dress. Tears trailed down his cheeks.

"Why did God allow this to happen to her?" he sobbed.

"I don't know, David, I just don't know," I said.

Why *did* God allow it? Why couldn't Annie have gone into a crisis while we were awake and could help her in time? Why didn't she die early that morning? What kept her hanging by a thread? I had rolled those questions over and over in my mind every day since her brain injury. I never got a clear answer, and I had nothing to offer David that would make it all better. I sat on the arm of the chair and put my arms around his trembling shoulders. Annie looked up at us, picked up another toy, tasted it and threw it across the room.

Chapter 29:

HELP...AGAIN

A crew of friends came over and painted Annie's room, installed closet shelves, a garage door opener for easy access for the wheelchair, and other handy home improvements. Bill's sisters, Susan and Janet, painted Olivia's room, too, because now that she and Annie were no longer in the same room, it seemed like a good time to freshen things up. Rick (the policeman in the ER) and his wife, Donna, bought Olivia a new, white iron bed too. Paint and new furnishings hopefully eased some of the memories of what had happened in her room early in the morning a few months before.

Friends, along with our families, held us together when Bill was sick years before, and they were holding us together now. Many people reached out and helped, each one's gifts seamlessly meshing with our needs. In March, my sister, Rebecca's 23-year-old daughter, Kate, flew out from her home in Texas a week or so after we brought Annie home. Kate had never met Annie, she had never seen her bright eyes, heard her singing, never watched her twirl in her pink, princess tutus. Perhaps seeing Annie lying on the living room floor with no strength to sit up as she looked out the window with a blank, brain-injured stare wasn't as jarring to her as it was to us...or maybe it was.

Intuitively, Kate seemed to know what to do to help Annie. Musically gifted, she walked in, sat down at the piano next to Annie, who lay propped up on pillows on the floor, and played for hours. Two pieces seemed to calm any anxiety Annie had—Chopin's Nocturne op.9, No. 2, and Comptine d'un autre ete-l'apre-midi, by Yann Tiersen. Mournfully, beautifully, the notes flowed from Kate's fingers onto the keys, washing peace over Annie and into our home. When Kate wasn't playing, sometimes I'd find her lying next to Annie, holding her, whispering in her ear, gazing into her vacant eyes as if willing her to come back to us.

Toward the beginning of summer, and after much intensive physical and occupational therapy, Annie sat up by herself. Friends and family pooled their resources to buy an adaptive tricycle for Annie to get outside and do something 'normal.' The bike was hot pink—a special request of the manufacturer from my nephew, Scott. It had a pole connected to the handlebars so I could pull Annie along, as well as a high back seat along with straps on her hips, trunk, and feet to hold her upright and safe. Annie loved getting on her bike and riding up and down our block, and would protest when I steered her back into our driveway. In September, I loaded up the bike in our van and took it to her school. Annie's one-on-one nurse, Moira, made sure she got a ride through the outside hallways and around the track as often as she could.

I held on to the (naive) belief that if we just gave Annie the right therapy at the right intensity she'd be as good as new within a year. I read that the first six to twelve months after a brain injury are when most recovery is achieved, and determined in my mind that Annie would regain the ability to walk, talk and eat within that time frame. Fortunately, our insurance paid for much of Annie's intensive therapy throughout that year, so when Sara, another family friend, organized a golf tournament in Annie's honor, I figured her recovery was imminent and that of course we really didn't need most of the money raised. So Sara donated the generous proceeds of the tournament to Children's Hospital for families in need. Which was a good thing. But after the first year came and went, I slowly realized that Annie's recovery had plateaued. In fact, without either ongoing intensive physical therapy or an act of God, Annie's ability to function was stalled at a 9-month-old infant level—and that was on a good day. Our insurance company no longer paid for intensive therapy by then, so we investigated a state program with funding therapy for people with disabilities called a "waiver." I never quite understood what they were waiving, but when you got on a "waiver," you received money to pay for respite care, therapies, and supplies like diapers. Because Annie's disabilities were deemed severe, she easily qualified for a waiver. Unfortunately, the state program wasn't adequately funded. This meant we were on a long waiting list with other equally deserving families but with no monetary help, at least not from the state.

Again, compassionate friends stepped in, and in January of 2008, my friend Andrea's daughter, Jennifer, organized a fundraiser auction for Annie as a high school senior project. Jennifer's father died of ALS a few years earlier, when she was only 13, so she understood the daily grief, as well as mental and physical intensity, of caring for a person like Annie.

The auction was held at our church, and included donations like weekends at ocean cabins, homemade quilts, and bountiful gift baskets. Jennifer also arranged for Annie to sit for a photographer who works with families and children with disabilities, so a beautiful, framed photo of Annie was displayed at the event. The church was packed with people that night, along with auction items covering tables around the sanctuary and decadent desserts displayed on tiered trays. Bill and I were overwhelmed with the generous response from everyone, many of whom we didn't even know, all there to help Annie.

As the auctioneer rattled off all the items and the bids rolled in, it soon became obvious everyone was offering far more than the value of each item. When all was said and done, $13,000.00 was raised for Annie's care. Bill and I sat in the back of the room—stunned by their generosity. All because a high school senior had taken her own hard experience as caregiver to a dying father to empathize with Annie's needs.

What did the money from Jenn's auction provide?

1. A registered nurse to babysit Annie a few times so we could go on rare date nights

2. Orthopedic shoes

3. AFO's (shoe orthotics our insurance didn't pay for)

4. A special-needs stroller with a sun visor so she could go on walks with us

5. An adaptive toilet in hopes that Annie could relearn that basic skill

6. Hippotherapy (horseback riding therapy) to strengthen Annie's core, with the hopes of enabling her to walk again

7. Occupational therapy to help Annie use her hands in constructive play

8. Physical therapy to strengthen her legs

9. A "Spio" suit (Compression leotard to counteract her sensory aversion)

10. A cedar log swing in our back yard for Annie to feel the breeze on her face.

The contributions of friends, family, and strangers helped not only Annie, but also us, lifting up our weak arms to bear the immense burden of caregiving for our severely disabled child. Their actions will never be forgotten.

Chapter 30:

MY YOKE IS EASY

Our son David relieved the burdens of living in our infirmary by playing basketball, and after Annie's brain injury he spent hours on the court of a local gym. One evening in early August he needed a ride back from the gym, so while Bill took care of Annie, I hopped in the van to go pick him up. As I turned the corner of our street and drove out onto the highway, I tuned into the local Christian radio station. Someone was talking about how Jesus rose early in the morning to spend time in prayer. The host asked, "When do you have a quiet time, early morning, late at night, or driving to work?"

Bill and I read the Bible and pray together every morning, and I pray before I hit the pillow at night...but is it enough? I wondered. After Annie got sick, I could barely string two prayers together. Bill and I were struggling to keep our heads above water with all the stress of her care, never mind the emotional needs of our other children. I felt this vague sense of guilt that my prayer life was on autopilot. Maybe I needed to ask God to help me spend more time in concentrated, focused time with Him.

The radio station switched to a commercial, so I reached over and tuned into the local classical station, turned down low so I could hear myself think ... or pray. My disconnected ramblings to God were interrupted by the sounds of soft, familiar music. I turned the volume up just a little. "...His yoke, is easy, and His burthen is light." I immediately recognized one of the choruses from Handel's Messiah.

Handel's Messiah in August? My attention was instantly riveted to the song coming from the radio.

"*His yoke, is easy, His yoke, is easy, His yoke, is easy—and His burthen is light.*"

The words washed over my mind and heart: *His yoke is easy and His burden is light... Was God speaking to me? Was He asking me to forget the works-based guilt about the quality of my quiet times, and just rest in Him?*

It suddenly occurred to me that God's Spirit *was* right there with me, and more importantly, was with me in my burden of caring for Annie. The thought stunned me, and I struggled to see the road in front of me as my eyes filled with tears. *God was with me! He was here bearing this burden with me!* As soon as I got home, I walked upstairs to our room, sat on the edge of the bed, grabbed my Bible, and looked up the verse in the gospel of Matthew that inspired George Frederic Handel's music in 1742: "Come to Me, all *you* who labor and are heavy laden, and I will give you rest. Take My yoke upon you and learn from Me, for I am gentle and lowly in heart, and you will find rest for your souls. For My yoke *is* easy and My burden is light."[25]

A yoke is made for two oxen, I thought. Jesus was on one side of the yoke, bearing this burden of caring for Annie with me, holding the weight on His shoulders. I wasn't alone and I didn't need to perform for Him. His yoke is easy, and His burden is light, and more than that, *He was with me.* What a precious gift for God to remind me that night that we were not walking this road of severe disability with Annie alone. He was Emmanuel, *God with us,* bearing the burden with us.

---

25   Matthew 11:28-30.

Chapter 31:

RETURN
TO ISOLATION

Often after a loss, there is an initial shock or crisis and then a leveling out into a new normal over time. For us that included a return to isolation. In many ways, this was a replay of what we experienced during Bill's illness. Disability is isolating. Sickness is isolating. When you don't feel good, you don't go out to see friends or family. You don't go to church. If people don't come to you, you are alone.

In addition, if one's disability has a socially awkward component, it is doubly isolating. For instance, Annie didn't eat so we couldn't take her out to restaurants. Even going to someone's house for dinner was uncomfortable because she didn't like to sit at the table in her wheelchair and do nothing. Also, because of the sensory aversion of her hands, she couldn't hold anything like food or a toy to keep her occupied.

Fortunately, Annie did like strolls in her wheelchair at the mall, and for the most part, that was our one socially acceptable pastime. One day

Bill bravely ventured out by himself for a mall stroll with Annie, and as he wheeled her through the mall she suddenly lurched forward, arms and legs stuck straight out in a frozen pose of brain misfires. Then as abruptly as it began, she flopped over into an exhausted heap. Annie's seizures were sadly commonplace to us, and Bill knew from experience that she'd come to in a minute or so. But for the woman whose shopping excursion was interrupted by Annie's contortions, seizures were most decidedly *not* commonplace. She bolted toward Bill and Annie screaming, "OH MY GOD! OH MY GOD!"

"It's okay, she's okay," Bill said, trying to calm the woman. Uninitiated to the myriad of emergencies we'd grown wretchedly accustomed to, the woman's shrieks drew a crowd of curious onlookers. Bill knelt to comfort Annie, then wheeled her away from the gawking of shoppers. Not surprisingly, he didn't take Annie out by himself much after that but made sure I came along to fend off any unwanted attention.

If going out with Annie wasn't always the most enjoyable activity, having friends over to our house usually was. Everyone who came to our home were truly messengers sent by God, encouraging us that we were not alone. Andrea dropped by now and then to dig weeds in our garden. Andrea's husband died of ALS a few years before, so she totally understood the isolation life-limiting illness brings. Now she was a caregiver again to her mother, Lee, who suffered from Alzheimer's. Andrea pulled out her gloves and tools and got to work, while Lee and I visited about nothing she'd remember. Annie positioned herself in the middle of the conversation, interjecting yells now and then. What a motley crew we were out there in the garden, but what camaraderie in bearing each other's burdens! Lee's big smile as she visited with Annie was a priceless moment. Those brief respites were little rays of sunshine on dark days.

Often, though, I couldn't shake the depression that came from caring for Annie. Days stretched into months that stretched into years of isolation. The changing seasons painted the maple tree in front of our house with shades of red, green, yellow and orange, and I could almost tell what day of the month it was by the color of the leaves. In spring, it sprouted yellow buds that morphed into tiny red leaves. By May, the red leaves turned light green and then a deeper forest green by midsummer. As the days grew shorter and the nights longer, the leaves glowed fiery gold and orange. Then one by one, they twirled to the ground and by November the tree stood bare, its gnarly gray bark groaning in the wind. A towering sentry outside our window, the old maple marked off the passage of time for me.

It stood silently outside our front door that cold, dark January morning when Annie's life hung between life and death, watching the paramedics scramble in with their equipment and bear the frail, blond patient out. In March when we brought Annie home from the hospital, its branches bent about in a stiff, spring wind. We thought a walk outside would be enjoyable for her, however, to Annie, the breeze was like a hurricane threatening to sweep her into oblivion. With a brain stripped of all sensory filters, Annie's body became rigid and her eyes froze in terror. We quickly retreated inside our house where the walls surrounded her again in quiet warmth.

In April, the sun danced through the leaves as a breeze rippled through them. That was the month when Annie began having drop seizures. The rehab therapist noticed that when Annie's attention was drawn to the sunlight strobing through the rustling leaves, she'd fall forward in a seizure. We tried to solve the situation by turning Annie so she couldn't see the tree outside that was so beautiful, and yet so dangerous, to her.

By December of 2007, almost a full year after Annie's brain injury, she began to smile again. The following spring, the little yellow buds covered the maple as they did every year, and the red leaves blossomed a few weeks after that. I snuggled with Annie in the recliner and looked out at the changing leaves and wondered *How long? How long will Annie be sick and not understand even the most rudimentary ideas? How many more years of watching the seasons change while Annie stayed the same?* Three years after her brain injury, the leaves turned orange again in the fall. And then winter came leaving the tree bare and gray, bereft of leaves.

The feelings of isolation evolved into a sense of chronic grief. I discovered that grief isn't an emotion reserved only for those who've experienced a loss by death. Grief also follows in the shadows behind anyone whose loved one has suffered any kind of physical or mental injury. Grief followed me as I searched for new toys to help Annie come out of her shell. All the princess toys she used to play with were no longer safe options. Barbie dolls and dress up princess outfits and her magical green wand she called a "focus,"...*Hmm, can't get any of those,* I thought. The tulle on the doll dresses overloaded her senses, guaranteeing an episode of vomiting. Barbie's hair also made her gag. After her brain injury, Annie could play with toys for infants who were 9+ months. Or 12+ months, if I was feeling adventurous. Nothing with flashing lights, though. Flashing lights triggered seizures. I'd stand there in the store a long time trying to find something appropriate, but nothing really was, so I usually walked away empty-handed.

Grief was also a factor in Bill's decision to leave the pastorate and the church where he worked before Annie got sick. The people there were our family. And Annie's friends were all there; friends she had played with in the nursery, and toddler room with Teacher Joy. But after she had her brain injury and I wheeled her into the classroom where all her friends were—all her friends who still could walk and talk and laugh—the pain was simply overwhelming.

One warm, summer Sunday, I wheeled Annie outside where a leader was playing Simon Says with the kids in the Sunday School class.

"Simon Says touch your toes." The kids all laughed and giggled as they touched their toes.

"Simon Says jump up and down." They jumped up and down.

"Simon Says spin around." I spun Annie around and wheeled her back into the church.

Another factor in Bill's decision to step out of ministry was the issue of time. Bill knew he needed to be at home in the evenings to help me with

Annie, and most meetings at the church were in the evening. Truth be told, his emotional and spiritual well was empty. He didn't have any words of wisdom for anyone who came in for counseling. People sat in his office wanting spiritual guidance, and Bill had none to give. Trusting God was something he was struggling with himself—how could he point the way for someone else? He told me after Annie's brain injury that he should apologize to every grieving person he'd ever counseled before she got sick. "I was so full of it— absolutely clueless to the pain of others."

So, Bill quit and we left. Not surprisingly, grief followed us to our new church. Foolish for us to think we could escape it. Standing behind Annie's wheelchair at the door of her new Sunday School classroom one week, I watched all the kids walk in, smiling and hugging their parents goodbye. I wheeled Annie toward the door and her teacher, Sarah, in her usual cheerful voice greeted her, "Good morning, Annie!" Annie's head hung down as she stared at the floor. *Must've just had a seizure*, I thought. *Or she's in the middle of an absence seizure. Or maybe she's just slow to respond.* Another wave of sadness rolled over me, and I turned and hurried down the hall and took a seat in the dark sanctuary, my red eyes safely hidden behind my glasses. As the worship leader asked us to stand, I tried to praise God for His mighty power—the power He seemed to be withholding from me. His power had healed Bill, but for some reason, He wasn't healing Annie.

There's a grief that takes up residence in your heart when your child has acquired disabilities. Acquired in the sense that one day they were fine and the next day they weren't. Or, over time, they lose abilities they once had. You don't get over these losses and pretend that they are differences like having brown hair or being tall. Reminders of what Annie 'used to be' hid around every corner. Even though I knew God *could* heal her, He was choosing not to, so far as I could tell. We existed in a land of no more words, no walking, no sharing a meal at the table. A land of dispensing medicines to give Annie energy, medicines to control seizures, medicines to bring down her high blood pressure, medicines to make her poop, medicines to make her sleep.

Sometimes I wondered if I ever forgot some medicine, would I go into her bedroom in the morning and find that she had died in the night? Bill told me later he always worried about that, too, and why he always wanted me to go into her room first. It was a heavy burden to know that the drugs I gave her every day were literally keeping her alive.

Chronic grief was a constant companion, keeping step with me, sitting down with me, going to bed with me and waking up with me. It never left. It was always there. Sometimes it hid in the background if my mind was otherwise occupied managing Annie's doctor appointments, medicine schedules or therapies, because when I was busy with those things, I didn't have time to think about how much we had lost.

One day I pulled out a couple of big plastic containers from under my bed, all packed with old family photos. What a mistake. As I sat there on the edge of the bed looking at the pictures from when the kids were younger; there was an innocence about them, a sense of promise and hope and future. Each child's birth, each Christmas, each birthday party, the years went by fast. After going through the stacks and stacks of photos from before Annie's brain injury, the promise and hope we used to have had been replaced by a permanent, dark cloud, an almost visible burden of loss on everyone's shoulders. Our hearts were broken.

I put the photos back under the bed and walked down the hallway and into the living room. Right then, God reminded me that someday Annie *will* be healed. Maybe not here on earth, but in heaven I knew God would heal Annie. Just for a moment, imagining her singing, dancing, laughing, talking, walking, running—*holding my hand again!*—brought immense comfort. But for the present, I clung to the hope that in spite of our brokenness, surely God was doing good things in our family. He was there with us. I saw Him through my kids as they read to Annie, talked to her, and held her. Those kinds of moments were anchors in my ocean of loss. Focusing on God's faithfulness kept the loneliness and grief at bay.

Chapter 32:

HE HEARS

Every Tuesday morning a couple of my friends joined me at our house for an informal Bible study. One day one of them asked me, "Do you ever wonder why, if God healed Bill, He doesn't heal Annie? And how do you live with that dichotomy?"

That was the proverbial $64,000 question, and no, I didn't have a clue as to the answer.

"I ask that question every day," I told her. "And every day I beg God that He would heal Annie."

What I didn't tell her were all the things written in my journal from a few weeks before. After praying so long for God to heal Annie, when I knew He could if He wanted to, I began to think He wasn't listening. *Lord, please heal Annie. I wonder how many times I've asked that. I've asked You for three and a half years to heal Annie. When will You listen to me and answer? Is she going to be stuck here forever? Not being able to eat or talk? Not being able to communicate? Lord, why don't You heal her? Why do You let her sit there in her messed up mind that doesn't work? Are You listening at all?* Journal, June 15, 2010.

The morning after I wrote that Annie woke up at 4:30 AM. I dispensed her morning medicine and tube feeding, parked her on Bill's lap on the recliner where they both fell asleep, and walked down the hallway to bed. As I headed back to sleep, God brought this verse to mind: (Jesus), "in the days of His flesh, when He had offered up prayers and supplications, with vehement cries and tears to Him who was able to save Him from death, and was heard because of His godly fear, though He was a Son, *yet He learned obedience by the things which He suffered. And having been perfected, He became the author of eternal salvation to all who obey Him.*"[26]

I sat up, turned on the light, and wrote in my journal: *After my rant last night, God reminded me that even though Jesus begged Him to spare His life, God did hear Him. Nevertheless, Jesus obeyed the Father and went to the cross. So I am reminded You do hear me and You have heard me begging You would heal Annie. But for whatever reason—and there is a reason—You have not healed her. But I know You hear me, even when You haven't healed her, and I need to quit wondering if You can hear me, because You do.*

With these verses, I was encouraged in a fresh and new way that God heard my prayers for Annie to be healed. He *heard* me. However, these verses revealed something else, too. Even as Jesus offered up prayers, cries, and tears to the One who could save Him from death, the answer was no—Jesus still had to go to the cross. As I meditated on that, I felt God was telling me that He was not going to heal Annie, and the answer for my prayers, cries and tears for her healing would also be "no."

This was a turning point in my acceptance of Annie's disability. I didn't want her to be disabled, I wanted her to be healed. But this verse reminded me that sometimes healing in this life isn't to be. Sometimes God calls us to persevere in suffering, sometimes for a very long time.

This is one of the main themes in the Bible, that Jesus, our High Priest, can relate to our pain and suffering. He cried, begging that His suffering be

---

26   Hebrews 5:7-9.

removed. And although He was heard by His Father, the answer was no, the will of the Father was that Jesus would go to the cross. "Not My will, but Thine, be done,"[27] was Jesus' humble conclusion that night in the Garden. It was God's plan from before the foundation of the world that Jesus' suffering, death, and resurrection pay for our sin.[28]

Although our suffering, and especially Annie's suffering, couldn't be compared to the sufferings of Christ, these verses in Hebrews gave me hope that 1) God heard my prayers, and 2) There was meaning and purpose in our suffering with Annie. Our light and momentary affliction wasn't pointless, but was sovereignly ordained for our good and His glory.[29]

---

27   Luke 22:42.

28   1 Peter 1:19-21.

29   2 Corinthians 4:17.

Chapter 33:

IDENTIFYING WITH THE WEAK

The practical outworking of God's "no" answer was that I let go of my insistence that Annie be healed and began to value who she *was* and not who she used to be. I learned to treasure and love her as an intellectually and physically disabled child. If Annie was going to be severely disabled, and God wasn't going to heal her, I needed to quit fighting Him over it and be content with what *was*, not what I wanted it to be.

Truly, Annie wasn't going to be permanently disabled anyway. Someday Annie and I will sit over a cup of coffee in heaven and talk about her brain injury and my caregiving. And when we have that conversation, I hope she says that 1) she felt loved by us, and 2) I did a good job taking care of her. Even though her brain wasn't working here on earth, it *will* work in heaven, and I will give an account for how I cared for her. What we do here on earth matters in heaven, even our caregiving. *Especially* in our caregiving.

These truths were modeled to me over the years by two friends, both mothers of special needs daughters. My friend, Jackie, demonstrated loving caregiving as she raised her daughter, Denay, who was born with spinal muscular atrophy. Denay's long, blond hair was usually tied up in ribbons and bows, and she looked like a princess in her wheelchair, almost like a carriage, on her way to a ball. Jackie seemed to take all of Denay's medical issues in stride and was determined that her daughter would live as full a life as possible. I thought a lot about Jackie and Denay when Annie first got sick. Jackie set the caregiving bar high.

My other friend, Carrie, mother to Amanda, who gave Annie the *With God All Things Are Possible* signboard, was another mentor to me. Amanda was born with significant physical and intellectual disabilities, but Carrie always has a smile on her face and upbeat attitude no matter what challenges she is facing. And again, Amanda is always well-cared for, rocking a cute bob and wearing coordinating outfits often decorated with red ladybugs. Both Jackie and Carrie modeled caregiving that gave their children dignity and confidence in a world that places an inordinate value on health and physical beauty. Special needs kids have enough hurdles to jump over. A little extra grooming in the morning can make those barriers a little less daunting.

Amanda's brothers were mentors to my sons too. They tenderly and patiently loved and cared for their sister, were proud of her accomplishments, and protected her in social situations. My boys watched them and learned.

We came to appreciate Annie's emerging post-brain injury personality. Her mischievous expressions slowly returned, with eyes that laughed, glared, and often communicated more than words could. If 60% of communication is body language, Annie spoke loud and clear. She eventually learned about five words: "No," was the clearest, followed by "Jack," "O-e-ya" for Olivia, "Hi," and "Yo-ee." Don't know if "Yo-ee" was "Mommy," but I decided it was. As we appreciated Annie and loved her as an intellectually and physically disabled child, we learned to value *all* people with disabilities. I came to understand that physically and intellectually disabled people don't just sit around waiting for someone to fix them. They simply live life! Although most people with any disability wouldn't turn down an offer for healing, they also can push forward and glorify God through weakness.

There is grace in weakness and grace in caring for the weak. Caring for Annie reminded me that Jesus bent down and took on *my* weakness. He could have stayed in the comfort and glory of heaven, but instead came down to our broken earth. He came as a helpless baby, then grew to be a man of sorrows and acquainted with grief. And ultimately, He was murdered on a cross, bleeding, suffering, and dying for us. He completely identified with our human condition that qualified Him to be a perfect Savior.

As Jesus identified with our weakness, God showed me the need to identify with Annie's weakness. Was it inconvenient for Jesus to come to earth? Was it uncomfortable? Did it cause Him sleepless nights? God graciously reminded me that anything I sacrificed for Annie—any quiet nights alone, any family vacations, any down time—paled in comparison to what Jesus did for me. I needed to be reminded of this constantly because caregiving *is* hard. I've had seven infants but caring for Annie was the hardest thing I have ever done. It was a daily floodlight on the selfishness of my heart.

Our kids also sat in this classroom of learning to identify with the weak. They learned not to fear anyone in a wheelchair, anyone who drools, anyone who throws up in the middle of the store, anyone who has seizures, and anyone who loudly repeats sounds that no one understands.

Our fifth son, Jack, came home from his job at the local grocery store one night and told me about a little kid who ran into the bathroom holding his hand over his mouth, slammed open the stall door, and just let loose. Jack leaned his ear toward the stall door and asked, "Are you okay in there, buddy?"

The little boy eventually opened the door, wiped his face with his hand, and quickly exited the bathroom. Then Jack walked over to the janitor's closet to get a mop to clean up the mess.

"What did you do?" I asked.

"No biggie," he said. "I've seen worse with Annie."

Peter shared that while driving in downtown Seattle, he passed a man with obvious signs of spasticity sitting in a wheelchair on the sidewalk. The man apparently tried to open his lunch and upended the whole thing in his lap. Peter stopped his truck, got out and helped the man retrieve and organize his lunch.

David and I were driving in our town one afternoon when we spotted a scowling man stomping across the street toward a young man David knew from school who had mental disabilities. David yelled to me, "Turn the van around, turn the van around!" Worried that we were about to get in the middle of something nasty—I had no idea the young man had disabilities—David was insistent, so I dutifully turned the van around. David jumped out, ran over, and quickly stepped between the two.

"He's cool, he's cool," David said to the angry man, as he steered him away.

"He just asked me to (sexually inappropriate thing)!!!"

"He's disabled—he didn't mean it," David explained, diffusing the altercation.

David saved the young man from getting beat up, and likely saved the angry man a night in jail.

You can't teach this stuff in school. Taking care of Annie changed all my kids. It changed all of us.

Chapter 34:

RETURN
TO DISABILITY

Along with our care of Annie, we tried to keep an eye on the mental and physical well-being of the main caregivers in our home: our kids and Bill and me. As I learned with Bill years before, and was now painfully reminded of, caregiving is hard work. It's a marathon, not a sprint, and our family, as her primary caregivers, needed to pace ourselves. That included respite care. Since we had no state sponsored respite care, family vacations were out; separate vacations were in. Now when I was growing up, money was tight and we never took vacations. Family vacations? What were those? But the intensity of caring for Annie meant that occasionally all of us needed to take a break to recharge. Typically, this meant that once a year, Bill took the boys for a few days somewhere fun, and I took Olivia for a few days away.

On one of those respite weekends, Olivia and I flew down to visit my brother in California. Disneyland may also have been on our agenda, I don't know. While we were away, Bill and Jack decided to take Annie out to a store filled with every guitar ever made, which back then was Jack's happy place. On that particular day, Annie was hooked up to her G-tube that connected a food bag to her tummy. After Jack carefully examined and played every guitar in the store, Bill wheeled Annie back out to the parking lot, opened the van door, disconnected the straps of her wheelchair and lifted her into her car seat. Her long G-tube, however, was caught underneath her wheelchair wheels. Back in California, I was in line at the drive-through at Taco Bell. My cellphone rang, I picked it up and quickly deduced that Bill might be going into cardiac arrest.

"Jean! Annie's tube just came out of her stomach! What'll I DO?!?" he yelled.

"Uh, I'm in line at Taco Bell. I don't know." I said. "Is Annie crying? Is she okay?"

"YES, she's okay, I think. YES, she cried a little...WHAT SHOULD I DO?"

"Well, I think you should call Carrie. Here's her number."

Carrie's daughter has a G-tube, and Carrie was the only person I knew who could help Bill. Even if he took Annie to a local emergency room, they probably wouldn't know what to do. G-tubes are only changed at clinic appointments during the day.

The problem with Annie's G-tube connection coming out is much like an earring coming out of a pierced ear. When there's no earring holding the hole open, it closes up. For earrings, that usually takes a week or so. For G-tube holes, it takes minutes to hours. We both knew that if someone didn't replace the tube connection immediately, Annie would have to endure another painful re-opening procedure.

After I hung up, Olivia and I prayed that all would go well. Bill called Carrie, who sped over to our house. Carrie, with a perpetual smile on her face and calm demeanor, immediately set Bill's mind at ease. She replaced the tube connection with minimal protesting by Annie and saved the day.

I was so thankful Carrie rescued us that day. My appreciation for Bill grew too. Not every father is as brave as he was, allowing me to take a break from caregiving. For any of us to take a break, the load on the others doubled. Bill was up for that. Our kids were too.

After we came back home from California, I decided to focus on quality-of-life goals for Annie. Like eating at the table with us. Because of her brain injury, eating at the table didn't happen for two reasons: 1) oral sensory aversion (a result of the brain injury), and 2) Annie didn't have a safe or big enough chair to sit in. I searched for suitable chairs for her, but oddly enough, highchairs are made for toddlers, not 7-year-olds. Her wheelchair was too low and didn't reach the height of the dining room table so that didn't work either.

The one place where I did find an appropriate chair for Annie was a medical equipment catalog and it cost as much as my first car. After a few unsuccessful tries to convince our insurance company that a highchair for Annie was an essential quality-of-life need, Annie's school occupational therapist sent a letter that secured a top-of-the-line highchair for us. The large red activity chair had comfortable padding, locking wheels so it could be moved around, and a wide tray with a raised edge that kept food from falling on the floor. It was perfect.

My next goal was to get Annie to eat; eating was her least favorite thing to do, maybe tied for first place with anyone touching her hands. We had been working on feeding therapy on an outpatient basis for three years, as well as every day at school, but her progress was less than stellar. So I decided to book her a room at a feeding therapy clinic for two weeks in late 2010. We hoped to decrease Annie's oral sensory aversion to food *and* decrease the calories of her G-tube feedings, hypothetically prompting an increase in her appetite.

Unfortunately, it didn't work.

The sensory filter in Annie's brain had been entirely decimated, so food was anathema to her. She didn't like to look at food, touch food, smell food, or God forbid, taste food. However, she would drink water. But add a drop of apple juice to the water? You'd wear it again. Annie also seemed to lack an appetite impulse, almost like she never seemed to get hungry. I wondered if that desire had also been destroyed by her brain injury. Be that as it may, after two intense weeks in the feeding clinic watching her lose weight she couldn't afford to lose and not making enough progress toward eating, we gave up.

The one good outcome of that whole episode was getting Annie's highchair. She could at least sit at the dinner table with us, even though eating wasn't part of the experience. I put carrot sticks, veggie straws and bits of food on her tray to try to lure her into picking something up and putting it in her mouth. And she did pick stuff up. But somehow the food never came near her mouth on its way to the floor. Our expectations necessarily went from "Annie will eat orally" to "Annie will sit at the table," and with that we called it good. Quality-of-life and social inclusiveness sometimes are the wins.

We moved along to the next mountain to climb which was Annie's living environment. We lived in a split-level house, with all living space and Annie's bedroom up two flights of stairs from our driveway. The stairs outside our front door led down to the van. Annie weighed between 45-50 pounds with clothes, orthotics and shoes on. Did she mold her body to mine as an infant would so she could "help" me carry her? Of course not. When I carried her up the stairs, her sensory aversion issues caused her to lean away from me, not toward me. Bill and I discussed the advantages of single story living with Annie's limitations, so I got to work searching real estate ads for single story houses. I spent hours and hours looking for any house that might work for Annie, our other kids at home, and our budget. Every night, I'd sit down and scour the Zillow ads for our area, then I'd widen the net to include a ten-mile radius of our town, then 25. I couldn't find anything we could afford that was on one level that would fit all our kids. So, I added that to my prayer list.

As Annie grew bigger—or longer—I should say, we also considered buying a wheelchair van. New vans cost around $50,000. Used ones were less, but if they were 10 years old, repair expenses had to be factored in. Yet without a single-story house to wheel Annie into, I still had to lift her out of the van and climb up the stairs to the main floor. An accessible van seemed like a waste of money, but I kept looking just in case we ever found that perfect single-story house. I never did find a one-story house or a wheelchair van. Because just like with Bill years before, we ended up never needing them.

Chapter 35:

INPATIENT

On February 17, 2011, Annie woke up sick. She had that familiar adrenal crisis look: pale, dark circles under eyes, fever, and she was vomiting. We had already given her a triple dose of hydrocortisone which she kept down, but I was afraid that wasn't enough. I sensed she needed an emergency injection, yet in the four years since her brain injury and subsequent diagnosis of Addison's Disease, I'd never given her the injection and was frankly afraid to do it myself. We decided to call the paramedics—*they'll be able to give her the injection,* I thought.

The medics arrived and one of them looked at Annie with a flash of recognition. As I described Annie's condition, and her brain injury from Addison's Disease, his eyes welled up. "We were here that morning," he said, glancing down at the place on the carpet where she lay four years before. He stared at Annie and I could almost see the videotape running through his mind: *blue, seizing, clenched jaw ... little blond girl so close to death. And this is what happened.*

I looked back at Annie, gathered my thoughts, and focused on what was going on right then. "We think Annie's going into an adrenal crisis. She needs an emergency injection of Solu-Cortef—it's right here." I held up the loaded syringe for him to see.

The paramedic backed up, sat down on the arm of a chair and said, "I'm not familiar with Addison's; can you tell me more about it?"

It suddenly dawned on me that I wasn't going to weasel out of giving Annie the injection. I needed to do it and do it fast. Filling in the paramedics about Addison's Disease and all things pertaining to adrenal insufficiency would happen on the way to the hospital. I gave her the shot and off we went to the hospital.

After we got there, Annie tested positive for strep. We found out later that she and some of her classmates in her special-ed class all got strep that week. The doctors, however, didn't think Annie needed to be admitted. So, we put Annie in the van and drove back home. Two days later, we went back to the hospital after Annie continued to get worse with vomiting, fever, and general malaise. She was admitted and subsequently also tested positive for Influenza B. Besides producing a bad cough, the influenza completely shut down Annie's already slow gastrointestinal system. Nothing stayed inside; whatever food she got through her G-tube came right back up. At seven-years-old, Annie weighed 43 pounds when she was admitted and quickly lost weight until she was down to a skinny 38 pounds. The doctors decided to give her IV nutrition, so an IV was placed in her little arm to deliver TPN—total parenteral nutrition, or nutrition through her veins.

Amazingly, almost overnight Annie revived. She gained weight quickly, back up to 41 pounds. Her skin became pink again. She even had enough strength to take long walks through the hospital in her Kidwalk—a walker that helped her move almost independently through the hallways. The change in her energy with the TPN was dramatic.

However, Annie's cough wasn't going away. An X-ray showed no pneumonia, but it did reveal that she had two compressed vertebrae, most likely a result of chronic undernutrition they said. Feeding Annie had been problematic since her brain injury four years before, but now there was clear evidence that even the food she got wasn't delivering the nutrition it should. But *why?*

Why was she chronically malnourished? And why did she seem to do so well on the TPN? I would have gladly continued the TPN, but the doctors cautioned us that it wasn't a good permanent solution, because IV sites are notorious entry points for serious infections. They recommended that a GJ-tube be placed in Annie's jejunum, or lower part of her gut to provide nutrition while hopefully also eliminating her chronic vomiting episodes.

I wasn't so sure about it eliminating the vomiting episodes. I knew that often her vomiting was a symptom of needing more hydrocortisone for her Addison's. Even if the food was further down in her GI tract, that wouldn't eliminate her nausea if she needed a stress dose. Frankly, I needed her to let me know when she was nauseated—that was one of the main ways I knew she was feeling bad. It wasn't like she could tell me she felt sick and needed more hydrocortisone.

Be that as it may, on March 4th, the surgeon placed a GJ-tube in Annie's lower intestine with a port to receive formula. She continued receiving TPN and the plan was to wean down on that when the rate of the formula going into the GJ-tube was enough for her to get all the nutrition she needed.

By Monday, March 14th, Annie's new GJ-tube wasn't yet up to the rate of food she needed to be able to disconnect the IV nutrition. As feared, she developed an infection, most likely from the IV site. This infection was serious and needed to be reined in with high-powered antibiotics.

On Wednesday, March 16th, after being in the hospital for a month, plans were made for Annie to be discharged. The doctors felt the infection was under control with the antibiotics and that Annie would recuperate well at home. When the nurse came into Annie's room with the discharge papers, Annie threw up. *Hmm,* I thought, *she probably needs more hydrocortisone. I'll give it to her at home. Maybe she'll do better at home. Kids often do better in their own environment, at home.* Yet a nagging thought in the back of my mind said she wasn't ready to be discharged. *But maybe she'll do better at home,* I argued with myself.

That afternoon we drove Annie home. She was happy to be around her brothers and sister and back in her own surroundings with her own toys and family. The next day a friend of mine came to help me with Annie. It was a good thing because Annie threw up repeatedly and had multiple drop seizures—all evidence that she was plummeting—and I appreciated the help. I didn't know if the GJ-tube wasn't working, or the antibiotics were making her sick or what. I just knew whatever was going on, Annie was going down fast. Fortunately, that day I had already scheduled a post-hospitalization follow-up appointment with her pediatrician, Dr. Brown, for 3 p.m. When Olivia came home from school, she helped me lift Annie into our van and we drove down to the doctor's office together. Dr. Brown had held our hand for the last four years, walking beside us as we tried to keep all of Annie's medical plates spinning. She had a professional interest in endocrinology and always gave me wise guidance in juggling Annie's seizures and Addison's Disease, while also respecting my own instincts about how Annie was doing.

By the time we got there Annie was looking very dehydrated with sunken eyes and a pallor to her skin. "Ooh, Annie doesn't look good this afternoon," Dr. Brown said as she sat on the stool. "She looks a little gray." Her eyes knit together in concern.

"She's been throwing up and seizing all day—I don't know what's going on," I said.

"Well, let's get an electrolyte draw on her and see. I'll write up the orders for the lab," she said.

I took the paperwork and followed Olivia as she wheeled Annie over to the lab in the next building. Susan, a good friend of mine from our church, worked in the lab. Susan is a kind, but no-nonsense phlebotomist, and after putting on blue exam gloves and assembling the syringe and tubes, she bent down next to the wheelchair to get a close look at Annie's arms. None of the veins looked particularly promising, but she chose one and gently and expertly tried to get a blood draw. Then she tried another. The other lab tech came over for one last try, but Annie's veins were too flat, and her protests were too loud for any of us to bear.

"I'm sorry, Annie," Susan said as she stood up and sighed. "I don't want to hurt her—these veins are just not cooperating." Susan looked down at Annie with sad eyes and then up at me. I could tell she was as worried about Annie as I was.

"It's okay," I tried to console her, while comforting Annie too. "We can drive down to the hospital and have their techs try."

After Bill got home from work, we drove Annie back down to Children's emergency department. They were able to get a lab draw, and after consulting with the doctors there, we asked them to readmit Annie. They agreed.

The next morning, March 18th, we were back in a new room, but with the same sick Annie. At around 9 a.m. the doctors gathered around her bed to assess the situation. I stood at the head of Annie's bed, a young resident stood on my right, and the attending doctor stood across the bed from us. The resident doctor opened the discussion: "Annie's labs this morning are normal and her systems are fine. I recommend that we make a referral to Behavior-Psych so Bill and Jean can learn how to deal with Annie's gagging issues."

"*Huh,*" I thought, as steam started coming out of my ears. Now the reality was Annie had gagging issues. *Behavioral* gagging issues. But she also gagged and threw up when she needed hydrocortisone. When a person who has adrenal insufficiency is sick, they require more hydrocortisone than a normal dose. A common symptom of needing more hydrocortisone is nausea, and although Annie had me all to herself when we were at home the day before, she still threw up repeatedly and had more than six seizures in the span of a few hours. Clearly, Annie was threatening an adrenal crisis, if not in one. Although I had stress-dosed her at home, she still was gray, gaunt, and dehydrated-looking, which is why we brought her back down to the hospital. That morning in the hospital Annie's lab work may have been absolutely normal. But she looked like death.

William Osler, (1849-1919) a British-Canadian physician, was one of four founding professors of Johns Hopkins Hospital. Perhaps Osler's greatest contribution to medicine was the establishment of the medical residency program, an idea that spread across the country and remains in place today in most training hospitals.[30] Osler said, "Medicine is learned by the bedside and not in the classroom. Let not your conceptions of disease come from words heard in the lecture room or read from the book. See, and then reason and compare and control. But see first."[31]

That morning, the older and wiser attending doctor must have seen my carotid artery pulsating, and quickly spoke up before I had a chance to respond to the resident's recommendation to call Behavior-Psych. "I think we need to schedule a little meeting—just (resident), Jean and me, so that Jean has an opportunity to be heard."

Bill was at work that day, but I needed his help in advocating for Annie. He left his office and drove twenty miles down to the hospital for the meeting later that afternoon. Bill, the two doctors and I all sat down in a one of the parent conference rooms. Bill acknowledged Annie's problems with her gagging behaviors but reiterated to the doctors that Annie required ongoing stress-dosing of hydrocortisone until whatever was wrong in her body cleared up. The attending doctor assured us that our concerns for Annie's care were

---

30 http://www.hopkinsmedicine.org/about/history/history5.html.

31 http://stanfordmedicine25.stanford.edu/blog/archive/2014/10-Osler-isms-to-Re-member-in-Your-Daily-Practice.html.

being heard and promised that whatever hydrocortisone Annie needed, Annie would get. The resident was silent throughout the entire meeting.

Afterwards, Bill drove home, packed up his overnight bag and headed back down to the hospital to relieve me for the weekend. This had been our routine for four years; I took the weekdays and Bill took the weekends anytime Annie was inpatient, which up until the last month had thankfully been a rare occurrence.

Before I left to go home, I told Bill I still felt stone-walled in getting the stress dose of hydrocortisone I felt Annie needed. I just didn't know where the problem was originating. Bill said he'd talk to Annie's nurse again about it when she came back in the room. I kissed him and Annie and reluctantly left for the weekend. I hated leaving Annie in the hospital, absolutely hated it. But Bill and I traded off so I could rest at home as well as spend time focusing on our other kids.

As I walked out of Annie's room and down the hallway with my luggage bag clicking on the tile behind me, I noticed the attending doctor sitting at a computer in an alcove. She stood up to say hello.

"Hi Jean, I was just writing down the notes of our meeting this afternoon."

"Great—hey, we've been asking the nurses for more hydrocortisone for Annie, but so far it hasn't come." I said.

"Who cares how much hydro we give her? It's not as if we're killing anyone with hydrocortisone!" she said emphatically.

"Well, that message needs to be communicated to the resident, because it's not getting through," I said.

"I'll do that right now," she assured me.

Exhausted, I stepped into the elevator and pushed the button to the first floor. *Why does advocating for Annie have to be such a fight?* I wondered. I walked out the door and climbed the stairs to the garage, my luggage banging on every step. Then I heaved it into the back of the van and headed for home.

Chapter 36:

THE DESCENT

On Sunday night, March 20th, I drove back down to the hospital to be with Annie. David and Jack came in, too, to see their little sister. They left in tears after seeing the dramatic change in her condition from only a few days before. Annie looked skeletal, bruised from all the IV's she'd had, and the circles under her eyes were darker than ever.

On Tuesday night Bill drove down to stay with Annie. Her Sunday School teacher, Sarah, also dropped by that evening to read to her. Bill told me later that she was visibly upset when she walked in the door and saw Annie.

By Wednesday the rate at which Annie could tolerate her GJ-tube feed was still too slow to keep her hydrated, let alone nourished. The doctors scheduled a surgery to place a central line into her chest for TPN but wanted to give her a day or two more to try to ramp up the rate of the GJ feeds.

That morning Annie seemed a little off to me, even more than usual. *I'll tell the nurse my concerns when she comes back in,* I thought. As I tidied the room, folded my blankets, and pushed the guest bed back against the wall, I noticed a tiny brown chickadee outside the window. It clung to the thin twig of a yellow shrub, pressing itself next to the glass. I watched it for a minute; it seemed to look back at me, tilting its head from time to time. It didn't fly away but perched there, watching.

I turned to get Annie ready for the day, brushed her hair and tied a pink ribbon in her ponytail. She didn't seem up for a bath, *I'll give her one later,* I decided. Just then, she slumped over in a seizure. Her seizures were usually short-lived, where her arms and legs would stretch out stiffly and then she would slump forward. Fortunately, she was in a soft, padded bed and wasn't in danger of hurting herself if someone was there to help her sit up right away. I sat down on the bed beside her and held her against my side. I thought I'd record the seizure in my notebook later.

My friend, Amber, also a mom of a daughter with special needs, was coming soon to sit with Annie so I could go down to the cafeteria for lunch. Annie required eyes on at all times, especially with these unpredictable seizures, and the understaffed nurses simply didn't have time to babysit. Amber's daughter, Molly, and Annie bore a striking resemblance to each other, so much so the kids in their elementary school often got them mixed up. Both had long blond hair and clear, blue eyes. Both were non-verbal and suffered from seizures. Two peas in the pod of severe disability.

Amber arrived around 11:20 a.m.

"Hey Annie! Hi, Jean."

"Hi Amber. Thanks for coming down! Annie just had a seizure a minute ago—she just isn't doing very well today."

"She doesn't look good; what's up with the hiccups?"

"She's been getting them off and on. I think they might be a sign she needs more hydrocortisone."

At least that was my theory. In fact, intractable hiccups are an early feature of Addison's disease.[32] It seemed like whenever Annie had hiccups,

---

32   //pubmed.ncbi.nlm.nih.gov/2616432/

she needed a stress-dose of hydrocortisone for her adrenal insufficiency. The doctors didn't seem to be impressed with my theories, though, and didn't want to increase her dose.

A few minutes later, the nurse came in with her noon dose of hydrocortisone.

"The doctor doesn't want to increase her dose right now, but I'm giving her the noon dose early."

Giving Annie her dose early is supposed to pacify me, I thought to myself. What Annie needed was a stress dose—a triple dose of hydrocortisone. I stood beside the bed, watching the nurse push the medicine into Annie's IV line and wondered why the doctors were being so stingy with the hydrocortisone.

Why Annie always required more than a regular dose of hydrocortisone for a kid her size and weight I didn't know, but the fact is she did. Her regular endocrinologist understood this, but her regular endocrinologist was out of town, and it seemed the endocrinologist covering for her was less than generous in his or her dosing instructions. *Maybe I should just mix up some more and give it to her myself,* I thought. It was in her backpack in the closet. *Would they send me to jail if I gave it to her? Why was it every time we checked her into this hospital, I felt like I was handing over the keys to my daughter's life?*

"You know, if she's going into a crisis, it'll be too late to give her..." I said.

"I definitely will relay your concerns to the doctor."

The nurse left the room, and I watched Annie to see if she'd perk up with the medicine in her system.

"So what do Annie's seizures look like?" Amber asked.

I demonstrated, "Her arms go straight out and she falls forward like this."

Amber snuggled up next to Annie in bed and got out her iPhone. Annie's attention turned to Amber's photos, and she seemed to perk up somewhat, so I left to grab something to eat. In less than an hour I was back in the room listening as Amber detailed what had happened while I was gone.

"I changed her diaper, and while I was washing my hands, Annie pitched my iPhone along with the book I had been reading to her. The book survived, but the iPhone screen cracked when it hit the floor."

"I am so sorry!"

"No problem. I think Molly cracked it before Annie finished it off."

Throwing objects was Annie's preferred play activity, so paying for a new iPhone screen, although a minor inconvenience, assured me she was still somewhat okay. However, her hiccups, which had gone away after the nurse gave her the hydrocortisone, were now back. Amber got up to leave, and I took my place beside Annie in bed. She burrowed into my side and slept off and on through the afternoon. The nurses came and went, and the conversation about more hydrocortisone continued to go back and forth between the doctors, nurses, and me. I should have screamed and yelled. I was too passive. I regret not having thrown a fit. I should have been the one throwing phones.

That evening, Sue, whom I met at a disability conference a few months before, drove up from her home in Tacoma to visit. Both mothers of seven children, Sue and I have affinities on several levels. Her sixth child, Luke, suffered a near-drowning accident when he was just 17 months old, so she understood the heartache of a healthy child suddenly becoming severely disabled. It was a sacrifice for Sue to get away from her own caregiving, much as it was for Amber earlier in the day. Why is it the busiest people are sometimes the most generous with their time? It's the caregiving sisterhood, women who know the emotional and physical burden of keeping their fragile little ones alive.

My plan was to ask Sue to help me bathe Annie, but over the hour, Annie was fidgeting in bed, grumpy, and not wanting to be touched. So we ditched that idea. David and Jack were there to visit, too, but it was immediately apparent to them that Annie wasn't doing well. Usually Annie was thrilled when her brothers came to see her, but she began shivering, and when the nurse came in to check her vitals, Annie was running a fever. Finally, the doctor authorized a triple dose of hydrocortisone. Sue prayed for us, gave me a hug and left. The boys hugged and kissed Annie, too, and left her room discreetly wiping their red-rimmed eyes.

A little later the night nurse, Hannah, came in, furrowing her eyebrows as she adjusted Annie's IV tubes. She had cared for Annie often these last six weeks and was worried about the fever. The doctor had ordered a urinary bag to check for a urinary tract infection, so another nurse, Jenny, came in to help place it.

After they took the tortuous bag off Annie, gave her the nighttime meds and helped me tuck her in, Jenny asked, "Do you mind if I pray for Annie?"

"Why don't we all pray together?" I said.

So Jenny, Hannah, and I stood around Annie's bed to pray. The nurses both put their hands on her, and I thought, *Annie's not going to tolerate that—she hates anyone putting their hands on her.* But she didn't pull away from them. When we were done praying, Annie was fast asleep. The fact Annie didn't resist should have sent alarms off in my brain that something was terribly wrong, but I just thought it was cool how their prayers had such a soothing effect on her.

The nurses quietly left Annie's room, and I turned to open the foldout couch, then laid out the stiff hospital sheets and blankets and my own pillow from home. Reaching up to close the blinds, I noticed my tiny, brown-winged sentinel was still at the window, keeping vigil on the same thin twig. Behind it, the yellow pom-poms on the kerria shrubs swayed silently in the evening breeze.

Chapter 37:

SWEET ANNIE

The next day Annie was more restless throughout the morning. Her face was puffy, and I noticed three dots on her face, one on her right cheek, one on her nose, and one on her left cheek. I thought it looked odd, so I took a picture of it and a short video to show to the doctors. I realized later the dots were petechiae; evidence of DIC or disseminated intravascular coagulation. I didn't realize it then, but a bacterial infection was taking hold in her body and dragging her down.

DIC is a rare, life-threatening condition which prevents a person's blood from clotting normally. It may cause excessive clotting (thrombosis) or bleeding (hemorrhage) throughout the body and can lead to shock, organ failure, and death.[33] It can be caused by infection as in Annie's case, which I found out later was a gram-negative bacterial urinary tract infection. The infection quickly morphed into sepsis, an infection throughout her body, effectively shutting down her vital organs one by one.

---

33   https://www.nhlbi.nih.gov/health/disseminated-intravascular-coagulation.

I called Bill. "What are you doing at lunchtime today?"

"Nothing—do you need me to come down?"

"Annie's really sick. Yes, I think you need to be here."

"I'm on my way."

I had a knot in my stomach and sensed things were spiraling down fast. I needed Bill to be there. And he needed to be here in case...

The morning nurse came in. I told her Annie needed more hydrocortisone. After a bunch of delays, and calls back and forth to the doctor, pharmacy and nurse, she came in with a triple dose of hydrocortisone. Annie grew more and more restless and I could tell she was plummeting.

"Why don't you check Annie's blood pressure and give me the medicine. I can give it to her while you're checking her blood pressure," I said.

"Yes, good idea," the nurse agreed.

The nurse gave me the syringe of hydrocortisone and put the blood pressure cuff on Annie's skinny arm. The nurse's eyes grew wide. Annie's blood pressure was 70/30. *I cannot believe this is happening,* I thought. The nurse ran out, yelling for a Rapid Response—an emergency call for all available medical staff to come the room immediately.

Bill sped 20 miles down the freeway, parked the car in the garage and got off the elevator in time to hear, "Rapid Response to room 2009! Rapid Response to room 2009!" As he tried to remember Annie's room number, a doctor ran past him. He followed quickly to room 2009.

Back in Annie's room, I took the syringe out of Annie's IV port and ran over to my bag to get my own emergency injection of Solu-Cortef, something I should have done an hour or two before. But by the time I had it ready, the nurse was back in the room with her IV injection of the same thing. The nurse quickly put the 100 mg. emergency injection of hydrocortisone into Annie's IV port as an army of doctors and nurses swarmed in.

Bill rushed in behind them and stood next to me as the staff feverishly began resuscitation efforts while simultaneously preparing to move Annie to ICU. We backed up and sat on the edge of the sofa by the window. Someone put a bag valve mask on Annie and started to manually force air into her lungs as she struggled to breathe. Annie's resident sat down beside us, out of breath, and briefly described what was going on. We listened, but there was no need for her to explain. We knew what was going on. Annie was dying.

One of the ICU doctors told us later that the doctors and nurses on the medical floor were shocked at how fast Annie went downhill. This is the frustrating daily reality for anyone with adrenal insufficiency. Any illness or trauma can be deadly in a matter of minutes if they don't get the hydrocortisone they need. In Annie's case, it could be debated as to whether more hydrocortisone would have helped her at this point. Even people without adrenal insufficiency die of sepsis.

The nurses clicked off the brakes on her bed, turned out the door and wheeled Annie down the hallway and into the elevator. Bill and I moved in slow motion, not quite believing what we knew was happening. We cleaned up Annie's room, gathered her blankets, toys and bag and took the elevator up to ICU.

We got off the elevator, walked past the nurse's station and there in Annie's room was her neurologist for the last four years, standing at the foot of her bed. Dr. Scott surveyed the dismal scene, peering over his glasses at Annie's motionless body. His arms were folded, one hand absently rubbing his chin.

About a year or so before, I had asked him about Annie's prognosis. Desperately needing him to predict Annie's future. I wanted some assurance that she would get better, be well, be healed and be herself again. With characteristic humility he said, "I'm a physician, but I'm not the Great Physician." He knew his limits, and he knew Annie required more than medicine to be healed. Dr. Scott was there in ICU the first day of Annie's brain injury; he held our hands for four years as we cared for her, and now he stood with us at the end.

We walked into the room, which housed two patients: a baby in an infant warmer to the left, and Annie in a hospital bed off to the right. On each side of her bed were towers of monitors tracking the drugs, blood and oxygen going into her body. We piled Annie's belongings onto the couch and crowded together on what little space was left. My friend, Gretchen, appeared with Jack and Olivia. I watched the nurses attend to Annie, hopeless that any action they performed could change her downward trajectory. After an hour or so, they moved the infant from Annie's room to another one down the hall. Gretchen left, then Jack. Olivia stayed and watched.

Annie was agitated and fought against the tubes coming out of her. The nurses gave her morphine to calm her and then shortly after decided to place her on a ventilator to help her breathe. They tried twice and finally wrestled the breathing tube in. The doctor noted to us later how she kept "breathing over" the tube, a grave sign her body still wasn't getting enough oxygen. Her arterial blood Ph level was 6.9. Over the course of the next six hours they couldn't get it over 7.1, and it kept going down to 6.9. She was acidotic, septic, and dying.

I walked out to the nurse's station and found Bethany, the young nurse who had cared for Annie so tenderly in the first week in ICU after her brain injury, and the charge nurse. "What does 6.9 mean? I want you guys to be honest. Some medical people have a hard time coming clean with the parents—I need you guys to be blunt."

"The 6.9 is her arterial blood gas level. Normal is 7.3. It means her organs aren't getting the oxygen they need," the charge nurse explained. Bethany wiped the tears from her face as she listened.

"We should talk to the doctor, then. Can you tell him we'd like to talk in a private room?"

The nurse looked around. "Yes, we'll get him...he's around here."

"Okay, we'll be in the parent conference room with Olivia."

We led Olivia down the hall and into the conference room.

I sat down beside her and Bill closed the door.

"Olivia, Annie isn't doing well—her body isn't getting the oxygen it needs. She could die...she might die," I said. The words coming out of my mouth seemed to cut Olivia's heart in two. Her eyes flooded with tears and she crumpled into my arms. I hated this—I hated what this was doing to my other kids, to us, and most of all, to Annie. Yet, Bill and I had always thought this time might come. We had numerous conversations with the doctors, with the palliative care nurse—we knew Annie was fragile. We tried to communicate this to our kids but seeing Olivia now, I wasn't convinced we'd done such a great job.

We passed around the Kleenex, got up, opened the door, and walked back down the hall toward Annie's room.

Bethany was there waiting for us at the nurse's station.

"I'm so sorry," she said, wiping her eyes. "Annie will be healed when she goes to heaven—she'll be able to walk and run and ride her bike..."

We hugged and soaked each other's shoulders with our tears. Then I looked past her to Annie's room and saw the doctor staring at the floor, waiting for us. I walked behind him and grabbed more Kleenex.

"You wanted to talk?" he asked.

"Yes, why don't we go back to the parent conference room?"

We walked single file back out of Annie's room, down the hallway to the conference room and sat down.

"We want you to be honest with us," I said. "The nurse said her blood gases were 6.9. How bad is this? Is she dying?" Somehow, I wanted him to confirm what I already knew to be true. The nurses had already leveled with us. But for some reason, the doctor wasn't as forthcoming.

"It's very serious…she could die—" His eye twitched as he continued, "…her blood gases haven't changed since 1:00 p.m. this afternoon, and it's been 6 hours. But I've seen kids worse than this pull out of it. The next 12-36 hours will be critical."

The doctor continued to describe details about her condition, most of which were a blur. I really didn't think she was going to pull out of anything, and I was frustrated he wouldn't tell us the truth. Maybe he was trying to give us hope, but the situation really seemed hopeless at that point.

Because he had said "12-36 hours" and he'd seen kids pull out of this, Bill and I made plans for me to sleep in one of the ICU parent rooms, and he would take Olivia home.

I wish now we had stayed with Annie. I wish now the doctor had told us to call our kids to come and see her. Maybe he thought we'd figure it out ourselves. Or maybe he was struggling with what was happening too. The fact was, we were all struggling with the grim reality of Annie's situation. The doctor, Bill, me, the nurses, we were all trying so hard to be honest with ourselves and look logically at what was happening in front of our eyes. And make logical decisions. And think logically. But we're human beings. The doctors and nurses are in the business to heal, to fix and to take care of. When those things aren't happening, when the patient isn't responding, how do they reconcile that in their minds? How do they step out of their own conflicted hearts to communicate with parents whose minds they can't read—parents who are teeter-tottering back and forth with their own emotions? *Let's all be grown-ups shall we?* we think. Yet we're also feeling human beings who want to believe that everything will all work out somehow. That night, though, things were definitely not working out.

I went back to Annie and kissed her goodnight.

"You'll call me if anything changes?" I asked the nurses.

"Absolutely. But don't worry. If we do call, it isn't necessarily bad news."

With their assurances, Bill left with Olivia, and I went up the elevator to the sleeping rooms—the sleeping rooms I'd stayed in four years before when Annie had her brain injury. I turned the key in the door, opened it and walked in. The tiny rooms were furnished with a bed pushed up against the wall, a small table, one dim lamp and an alarm clock. The hospital phone hung on the wall, silently threatening by its very presence. I sat down on the bed and recalled the details of Annie's crisis from the January morning of 2007. In those first days after her brain injury, the trauma of that morning played in an insidious loop in my mind, and was my first thought each morning, my last at night. My doctor had prescribed sleeping pills as soon as he'd heard what happened to Annie. "You're probably going to need these," he said.

Now here I was again in the little sleeping room where it all began, and where it seemed to be ending. *"Lord, please be with Annie now,"* I whispered. *"Please be with us. Please help us."*

I couldn't sleep and finally got up, took a shower and dressed. At 5:15 a.m. I called down to Annie's room.

"We're having trouble keeping Annie's blood pressure up...things aren't looking good," the nurse said.

"I'll be right down."

Before I got on the elevator, I called Bill. "Annie's not doing well. You need to come now."

"I'll be right there."

Bill woke Olivia, David and Jack and called Taylor, Peter and Andy. With the exception of Taylor, and Andy and his fiancé, Naomi, who were rushing from Portland to get there, they all arrived within half an hour.

I took the elevator down to ICU and walked into Annie's room. Her hands and feet were cold, and her fingers and toes were dark. The machines were keeping her alive and I knew she would die as soon as they were turned off.

This is it, I thought, *the day I knew would come is here too soon.*

I set my bag down on the sleeper sofa. The nurse looked up from her charting. "Is there anything I can get you?"

"Yes, I think we're going to need about six boxes of Kleenex."

"I'll get them right now," she said, then disappeared out of the room.

Jack, David and Peter walked in, followed by Bill and Olivia. We all surrounded Annie's bed, taking turns holding her hands, her face, touching her hair, whispering in her ear. I didn't know if she could hear us, but we spoke as if she could. The nurse stood at the end of the bed, eyebrows knit together, watching the monitors. Suddenly, she prompted us to come near. "It's getting close," she said, glancing up at us. Annie's blood pressure was falling quickly. We squeezed in as much as we could, given all the tubes and IV's coming out of her.

The nurse noticed our attention was drawn to the monitors, trying to make sense of them instead of to Annie. "Do you want me to remove the IV's?"

"Yes, please."

She turned off the monitors, and both nurses quickly removed all of Annie's IV's.

We hovered around. Watching. Crying. Waiting.

Annie seemed to be slipping away before our eyes.

"Do you want us to remove her breathing tube too?"

"Yes."

With Annie's breathing mask gone, I bent down to kiss her little bruised face. *Sweet Annie, I love you so much. I'll see you in heaven very soon.* Her eyes opened briefly; then she was gone.

One of the nurses stepped out of the room and a short time later the doctor came in with a stethoscope and placed it on her chest for a few moments. "I don't hear anything," he said, then he turned and walked out. It was 7:35 a.m.

Chapter 38:

WAKE

Before Annie had her brain injury, she used to sing *Here is Our King* by David Crowder from her car seat in the back of our van while we ran errands together. At 3-and-a-half-years old, she knew the words to the song, but especially enjoyed the chorus about Jesus bringing us back to Him. And on March 25th at 7:35 in the morning, Jesus did come to bring Annie back to Him. After six weeks in the hospital and many complications, she died surrounded by her brothers, sister, Bill, and me.

The nurses told us we could stay in the ICU room with Annie as long as we wanted. We called our family, Bill's parents, sisters, brothers-in-law, cousins and many friends—pretty much everyone who was within driving distance made the pilgrimage to the hospital.

You could say it was a modern-day wake. People don't do those anymore, where the deceased is laid out on the kitchen table, and the neighbors and family all gather around for three days to mourn their loved one. There was a purpose to those rituals though. Making space in life to grieve a loved one is a gift. Our Western culture avoids all things pertaining to death and dying. *Call the mortuary to come and get the body as soon as possible. No services at their request.* Cremate and bury them before anyone has a chance to shed a tear. However, when we don't embrace death and loss, giving grief the time and space it deserves, it has a way of finding us six months, a year, five years down the road demanding our attention in other ways.

Thankfully, the hospital gave us as much time as we needed to gather around and say goodbye, so we settled in. As far as I was concerned, Annie had just stepped into heaven so she was fine, which was an indescribable relief. I would never worry again if she had enough hydrocortisone. She was finally healed. But she was gone from us. Death is the last enemy to be destroyed, as 1 Corinthians 15:26 says. And death is a cruel foe.

My kids, all of them so much older than Annie, and now with faces wet with tears, shoulders bent over with heartache, looked even older. *What could I do to help them?*

"You can climb into bed with Annie if you want," I offered.

David didn't hesitate and climbed in first, all 6'7" of his frame enveloping his precious sister as his tears spilled onto her hair. Olivia then took a turn and snuggled in close for one last hug. I stood next to the bed, resting my hand on Annie's chest, still warm with the life that had just left her, and leaned in to smell her hair, the skin on her neck, and whisper into her ear. *Sweet, sweet Annie. I'll see you soon. I'll be there soon.*

The Child Life staff peeked in, young professionals who used to bring toys for Annie to play with when she was inpatient. Their other job, I found out that day, is to help grieving families create remembrances of their little ones who've died. They tiptoed in like church mice, asking permission to make handprint and footprint keepsakes.

"Of course," I said, "thank you so much."

They went about their work, speaking in hushed tones as if to not waken the little princess lying in the bed. They made a garden stepping stone with her footprint, hand molds, and two round glass Christmas ornaments with her handprints. Tucked inside the box with the glass ornaments they placed two pink satin ribbons with letters looped through them that spelled *Annalee.*

As news circulated in the hospital that Annie had died, many of the doctors and nurses who cared for her asked if they could come in and say goodbye. They trickled in, heads down, gripping tissues, hearts heavy. The resident with whom I'd had so many frustrating conversations came in, sobbing, unable to speak. A thought went through my mind that Annie might be the first patient the resident had ever lost. I reached out, hugged her and whispered, "You'll be an excellent doctor." And I believe that. Annie taught each doctor who cared for her so much about adrenal insufficiency, brain injury, seizures, and little girls who defy explanation; little girls who don't fit neatly into medical textbooks.

Bill's family came in and the double room was filled from end to end. Everyone made their way to kiss Annie goodbye, and then we gathered around her bed to commit her to the Lord. Bill took his place at the head of her bed and we all held hands and prayed as our eyes and noses dripped onto the floor.

After his family left, Bill and the kids and I gathered around Annie's bed one last time. Bill wanted to bless our children and create a memory of comfort in their minds that would remain with them, hopefully, for the rest of their lives. He gazed down at Annie's body and then around at our children's anguished faces.

"Your mom and I want to thank you for everything you did for Annie these last four years. It was hard, really hard. But your unselfish attitudes, your help, and your love for her through it all…thank you. You did a good job. We love you, and God loves you, and He'll be with us as we miss Annie."

With hands gripped tight and heads bowed, we wept our way through Bill's prayer.

"God, thank you for Annie's life. Thank you for each day we had with her—" Bill paused, hardly able to continue. "Thank you, thank you that Annie is healed and in heaven with You now. Please comfort us in our grief and sadness. Help us to trust You until we're with her in heaven again. Amen."

With that, we hugged each of our children, and they slowly slipped out the door, leaving us with Annie's body for a few more moments. It was now almost 1 p.m., but Bill and I were conflicted about leaving her there with the hospital staff all by herself. One of us had been with her almost constantly since her brain injury four years before. Annie's spirit may have departed her body, but the thought of our physical departure from her left our hearts in shreds.

Bill and I tucked the red and yellow sock-monkey rag quilt that my niece, Lorraine, had made around Annie's body. Then we gathered her books, stuffed toys, and food backpack and walked into the hallway to wait for the elevator. The doors opened and we stepped inside, and I wondered if the people standing beside us could sense that our daughter had *just died*. *You know, my 7-year-old daughter, Annie, died this morning,* I wanted to tell them. *We just left her upstairs in ICU. She's not coming home with us anymore. Can you see in our faces that our daughter is dead?* Bill and I were no longer parents of a severely disabled child. We were grieving parents. The elevator door opened, we turned our parent badges in at the front desk and walked outside alone into the cold March air.

Chapter 39:

THE DAYS AFTER

Bill had a visceral response to Annie being out of his sight, out of his realm of responsibility. It was his job to be the determined guardian, after all, and who was guarding her now? It left him with an extreme sense of anxiety and complicated his grief. He kept asking me, "Where do you think they're taking her body? Do you think she's in the hospital morgue by herself, or do you think the funeral home has her now? Where do you think she is?"

Those first few days were a tug of war in his mind between his very real feelings of wanting to continue in his role as Annie's guardian and protector, and the reality that "she" wasn't in her body anymore, so what difference did it make? Annie may have made the transition between death and life in heaven in an instant, but our transition from caregiving parents to parents with empty arms was going to take time...a long time.

Bill never experienced the death of someone close to him. This was all new and awful territory for him. I had experienced the loss of my mother and my sister so had a better idea of what lay ahead. Our other children never had suffered this kind of loss either. Although I tried to coach them as to what to expect, those early hours, days and months of grieving were excruciating for them. Looking back, we probably all should have gone to grief counseling. When I suggested it, no one was interested. "Oh, I'm fine. I don't need that." Well, you do. We all do.

There were many hours that first week where we would just gather in our living room, sit together and talk. No one seemed to want to leave the living room. We just sat there. Energy drained out of us, and a weight, almost a palpable heaviness, pressed us into the cushioned sofas. Yet no one wanted to leave our cocoon of communal grief. Then it seemed we couldn't leave it; sitting together made the weight easier to bear.

The house was quiet without Annie. Instead of her constant chattering, a painful silence enveloped our home. I walked down the hallway and slipped into her bedroom, looking at all that had been hers. Everything was as we'd left it when she was here the last time. A blanket tossed onto her hospital bed. Her hair bows and brush on the dresser. I picked up one of Annie's ribbons and touched the blond strands of her hair still tangled in it. My eyes stung as I put the ribbon back down on the dresser, walked out and closed the door.

Bill and I needed to tie up the rest of the arrangements at the mortuary, so I told the kids where we were going. "We need to meet with the funeral director today, so someone needs to be here to take care of An—" I said to no one in particular. Oh. Right. No one needs to take care of Annie. Bill and I can get in the car and go to the funeral home alone. Emotions of loss, guilt, sadness and relief all mixed up together.

Our house filled up with flowers and food. Lilies, pink tulips, white roses. Food and flowers spoke comfort to me. Might not be everyone's love language, but it was mine. We felt God's steadfast presence in our grief through the words and actions of our friends and family. God showed me His presence in other ways too. A few days after Annie died I was standing at my kitchen window looking at the perpetual calendar on the windowsill, *"Unto The Hills,"* by Billy Graham. It was still open to March 25th, the day Annie died. The devotion on it read:

The Christian should never consider death a tragedy.

Rather he should see it as the angels do:

They realize that joy should mark the journey from time to eternity.

The way to life is by the valley of death,

But the road is marked with victory all the way.

And on the bottom of the page was the verse from John 11:25:

"I am the resurrection and the life;

he who believes in Me, though he were dead, yet shall he live."

God reminded me right then that He had planned each of Annie's days, including the day she would die. As Christians, we know this theoretically. But here, on a pre-printed calendar, God reminded me that He is sovereign over every detail of our lives. What an incredible comfort that was to me at that moment!

I also felt God's reminder that He was sovereign over the morning of Annie's brain injury when I read that verse from John 11. It was the verse I'd taught the women three days before Annie's brain injury from the adrenal crisis in 2007. Throughout the previous four years, I'd struggled with this. *How could He have seen her in her bed, struggling for breath, descending into a coma, and not done anything? Why did He let that happen?*

Lazarus' sister, Martha, had the same question. "Lord, if you would have been here, this wouldn't have happened!" Just as Lazarus' sister struggled with his illness and death, so I struggled with Annie's brain injury. And here, thousands of years later, in the same words with which Jesus comforted Martha, He also comforted me: "I am the resurrection and the life; he who believes in Me, though he were dead, yet shall he live." I knew it was true: Annie was alive.

Yet, even though she was alive in heaven, we still were here on earth having to attend to the details of her death. The last time Bill and I met with a funeral director we were making arrangements for him more than ten years before. Now here we were again, sitting in a funeral home, only this time we were picking out a small white casket for our 7-year-old daughter. We chose a burial plot near an ornamental plum tree that blossoms into clouds of pink in March of each year.

Another detail that needed to be attended to is that Annie needed something to wear, so Olivia and I went shopping. And as God's providence would have it, Easter dresses filled the racks of all the stores. *How appropriate Annie would wear a dress made for Resurrection Sunday,* I thought. We found a soft, apricot-pink dress with a tag that said *Cinderella,* an ivory cardigan sprinkled with tiny pearls, and dainty white gloves to conceal the dark bruises on her hands. An organza ribbon for her hair and white socks with ruffled cuffs and bows completed her outfit, all provided for with the remaining funds from Jenn's auction a few years before.

Decisions about what I should wear to Annie's funeral seemed trivial but attending to details provided me a break from crying. Plus, I needed shoes for the simple black dress I decided to wear. The shoe department wasn't particularly busy that day and it wasn't long before the salesclerk came out with a stack of boxes.

"Are these shoes for a special occasion?" she asked.

Widow's garb would have been a helpful social cue for me to have on right then. Some visual sign that might eliminate what would be the first of a hundred awkward conversations.

"I need them for my daughter's memorial service."

"Oh, I'm so sorry," the clerk said, her eyebrows furrowing. "Can I ask what happened?"

"She had a brain injury about four years ago from undiagnosed Addison's disease. Then she died Friday from complications of the flu."

"Oh, I'm so sorry," she said again. "How old was she?"

"Almost 8 years old."

The clerk's eyes immediately filled with tears. She looked down and wiped her eyes. "She had a brain injury?"

"Yeah, the brain injury caused seizures ..."

"I have epilepsy, too!" she interrupted in a gesture of solidarity.

I listened numbly as she shared her story. Her intention was no doubt to let me know she could relate, but all I could think of was, *"Yes, but you're alive."* Feeling fragile and self-centered, I had no emotional energy to give back to her. My compassion bucket was empty. And, of course, this is a risk when sharing your grief with anyone. People may or may not give the comfort you're looking for. When they don't, it's an opportunity to extend grace their way, which I must admit I didn't feel like doing. We are all broken and we all need comfort. We carry our losses as knapsacks on our shoulders and limp along, often thinking our burden is the heaviest one of all.

After I chose some black patent pumps and paid for them, she came around the counter and hugged me. As she stepped back, I noticed her eyes brimming with tears. *God, give me your grace and glory. I need your grace and glory,* I thought to myself.

The details of planning Annie's memorial service included the option of an open, closed, or no casket service. Bill and I decided on an old fashioned open-casket funeral, but I was concerned the mortuary wouldn't be able to cover the significant facial bruising from the sepsis. Providentially, my daughter-in-law at the time, Cris, was a makeup artist so I asked her if she might be willing to help the mortuary with those details. She had never done anything like that before, so she hesitated at first, then agreed. She told me later what an honor it was to sit with the mortuary makeup artist as they prepared Annie's body. They took turns working as Cris shared about Annie and as each curl and ribbon was set in place.

It was important to me that every part of Annie's memorial honor her life and did its job, whatever *it* was, to erase the memory of her painful death. To be honest, anything we did to mourn her or celebrate her life was eclipsed by an awareness that she wasn't here with us, but in heaven with Jesus. Yet as mere mortals who grieve we wanted to honor her here on earth.

I wanted Annie's party to be a gathering that reflected her feminine little self. Pink and purple were her favorite colors, as every girl's often are, and if Annie would never go to the prom or walk down the aisle dressed in white, we needed to throw a celebration she'd have loved. Frankly, I have never understood why anyone wouldn't want a memorial service. Friends and family singing, laughing, crying together…who would pass that up? Even my dad's funeral, the guy who abandoned us when I was 8 years old, was somehow delightful. Reminiscing with the elderly ladies from the church of my childhood, friends of my mothers, who drove three hours in a snowstorm because they *knew Ann's kids would be at their dad's funeral.* What a hoot! And the food! Western Pennsylvanian East European cookies, nut rolls, sandwiches, it was like a time warp back to my childhood. Rather than being depressing, funerals can be a touching grand finale, wrapping the characters (always plenty of those) of a person's life in a big, warm hug. And that's just how I wanted Annie's memorial to be.

Not surprisingly, making Annie's arrangements brought back memories of my mother's funeral service. Chemotherapy had not been kind to my mother, and I looked forward to finding comfort in an embalming makeover of sorts for her. For me, a good job by the mortuary meant Mom would look a whole lot better in her casket than she did in that hospital bed before she died. In fact, just to make sure they had performed their cosmetic duties well, my sister, Marilyn, and I sneaked in to see her the evening before the official viewing.

We drove to the mortuary, slipped past the unattended front desk, and tiptoed into Mom's reposing room as if we were there to steal the Hope Diamond. The gray casket was open and Mom was in it. So far, so good. Mom's blond-white hair was styled just like the picture we had provided them, and she wore the soft, pink blouse I'd sewn for her. Then Marilyn and I simultaneously spied the same wretched blunder.

"*Orange lipstick?* Mom *never* wore orange lipstick. That doesn't go with the pink blouse at all!"

"Why would anyone put orange lipstick on her?" Marilyn asked. "Didn't we tell them to use pink?"

"They should have known to put pink on her; she's *wearing* pink."

"And what's that?" Marilyn asked as she reached over, delicately plucking out a wayward eyelash.

"I don't think we can fix the orange lipstick. We should just tell them to do it."

"Well, they'll need to do it before Aunt Jane sees it," Marilyn said.

On our way out, we brought the lipstick gaffe to the attention of the staff, who assured us pink would be on Mom's lips the next morning. As I recall, my aunt found out about our shenanigans later, which threatened to put her in an early grave too. I think there are things you just have to do and ask forgiveness for later. But what do I know? Well, I know my mother would never wear orange lipstick. I know that.

The morning of Annie's visitation day, Bill and I drove to the funeral home and pulled into the parking lot. The drizzle of an early morning spring shower sparkled on the daffodils just outside the door. We walked in and were greeted by the funeral director.

"Mr. and Mrs. Sullivan? How are you this morning?" she asked. Her kind eyes were filled with compassion. It was obvious the mortuary staff didn't much like children's funerals, either.

"We're okay, thanks," Bill lied.

"Well, let me show you where we have Annie. She's received quite a few flowers already."

We followed her down a long hall with windows overlooking weeping cherry trees on the right, and reposing rooms on the left.

"She's right in here," the funeral director said as she gently opened the double white doors into a softly lit room. Bouquets of pink roses and lilies delicately scented the room while comforting hymns I recognized from my childhood played quietly in the background. Bill took my hand as we stepped inside and peered down into Annie's casket. Her perfectly shaped eyebrows, long curled eyelashes, tiny upturned nose and heart-shaped lips; a solemn beauty surrounded her even in death. Her white-gloved hands were folded neatly on her lap; a tumble of blond ringlets fell around her face and onto her shoulders.

"Annie *never* allowed hair near her face!" Bill and I suddenly said almost in unison. With her sensory aversion, even a wisp of hair on her cheek provoked loud protests. As we stared down at our sleeping princess, what was remarkable wasn't what we saw, but what we *didn't* see. Annie wasn't seizing, she wasn't throwing up, and she wasn't struggling anymore. She was perfectly at rest.

"Lord, thank you for Annie's life," Bill prayed. "Thank you for giving her to us for just a little while. Thank you that she's with You now. Please comfort us as we miss her and tell her we love her and can't wait to see her again. Amen."

Chapter 40:

GATHERING
TO REMEMBER

We didn't have a videographer or official photographer at Annie's memorial service. I thought it would be lacking in taste. Yet it's a decision I somewhat regret. I thought it would be enough to commit the record of Annie's going away party to my memory. "To be in the moment," as they say, and soak up each second of the last few hours of her little self being with us, because I knew it would be a very long time before I saw her again. Maybe that was a good decision, maybe not. But that's what we did.

Bill and I sat down with Pastor Steve a couple days after Annie died to go over logistics.

"We'd like you to do the service."

"This'll be my first," Steve said as the color drained from his face.

Steve and Bill had worked together for six years, Steve the youth pastor and Bill, the executive pastor at our church. Steve's son, Jackson, had been born about a week before Annie, and the two of them shared every developmental milestone until Annie had her brain injury. Twenty years younger than us, Steve and his wife, Carla, were on the front end of their childbearing years and we were on the back end. They were witnesses to our four years of loss and grief and severe disability. Now Steve was the senior pastor at the church. We knew he'd do a great job with Annie's service.

This was the church Bill had served in when Annie had her brain injury and they graciously offered to host Annie's memorial. We were humbled and very grateful. We arrived a couple of hours before it began and were welcomed by an army of cooks, cleaners, and flower arrangers. So many people we hadn't seen in a long time came to support us with their generous acts of service.

My friend, Maurita, was in the foyer putting the final touches on four tables covered with Annie's photographs, artwork, favorite books, toys, and blankets. Maurita's son, Lucas, and Annie had shared many toddler playdates, and Maurita had a bulging file of Annie/Lucas photographs. As she guided me through each vignette, I noticed her lip quiver and her eyes well with tears. It began to dawn on me how many others there that day had lost their precious Annie too.

A line formed behind the two guest books, and in another hour the church was packed. Everyone who ever knew and loved Annie was there. Our families, her friends from school, their parents, para-educators, teachers, doctors, nurses and many who prayed us through her short life of health, sickness and now death. A few of the parents of special needs kids quietly pulled me aside to make sure it was okay for their kids to be there. It bothered me that they felt it necessary to ask, because after her brain injury, Annie's voice was often the loudest in our church. Did anyone ever ask *us* to leave? *Never.* Was it okay for her friends to be at her funeral? Absolutely. I wanted them there. In my mind, they were the guests of honor. Jesus said as much to the disciples when they wanted Him to shoo the children away. "Let the little children come to Me and do not hinder them, for to such belongs the kingdom of heaven."[34]

After everyone was seated and pink-ribboned programs were clutched in laps, the funeral staff walked over to close Annie's casket. *Oh dear, this is it,* I thought, *this is the last time I'll see her. I need to stand up and say goodbye.* It happened so suddenly, but Bill and I stood and walked the two steps up to reach Annie, bent over and kissed her cheek then sat down. The mortuary staff closed the casket, then Pastor Steve stood up to open the service. Sweat beaded on his forehead as he glanced down at what lay before him. Bless his heart, I just wanted to run up and give him a big hug. *Steve, don't you know God is helping us bear this?*

God's grace is sufficient at the moment you need it, not before. He never seems to send the ability to go through trials ahead of time. During Bill's illness, and Annie's sickness and death, God gave us His power to endure each trial at just the right moment. He was always on time. To worry or wonder, "Oh, what would I do if this happened to me?" is a pointless exercise, because God gives us His grace *at the moment* we need it. John Piper explains this simply as "future grace." "Future grace is God's power, provision, mercy, and wisdom—everything we need—in order to do what He wants us to do five minutes, five weeks, five months, five years and five thousand years from now."[35]

We live on the broken side of heaven, but Emmanuel, *God with us,* gives us His grace to walk through the valley of the shadow of death. The day of Annie's memorial service, His grace filled up the church from floor to ceiling, from wall to wall, and wrapped Its comforting presence around my heart.

God's grace also worked through the many individuals who contributed their gifts to honor Annie through music. Our sons Peter, Jack and

---

34   Matthew 19:14.

35   http://www.desiringgod.org/interviews/what-do-you-mean-by-future-grace.

Andy put together the band, with friends Molly on piano and Luther, (my nurse-friend Pam's husband) on bass. Peter and Andy took turns on the drums, and Jack played lead guitar.

Sarah, Annie's Sunday School teacher, was the first to speak. Sarah had courageously welcomed Annie to her class for two years, even though Annie was developmentally light years behind the 3- and 4-year-olds in her class. Prior to working with Annie, Sarah didn't have any experience working with children with special needs, much less one who sat in a purple wheelchair and wore a pink padded seizure helmet. But Sarah bravely opened her heart to Annie. "I'm so thankful I was able to visit Annie, and read to her in the hospital the Tuesday before she died. I just didn't know it would be the last time," she said as she wiped the tears from her cheeks.

Miss Vickie followed next. Vickie and her husband, Jack, were like Annie's other parents, and babysat her frequently before her brain injury. When we were in Ireland, she told me that Annie's favorite place to be was covered in bubbles in her whirlpool tub. After Annie's brain injury, Vickie held her during her brain injury storming, whispering songs, reading *The Napping House* and praying into her tormented ears. Now Vickie stood above her casket weeping, yet thankful that her sweet Annie was healed at last.

Olivia decided to speak at her little sister's memorial too. She marched confidently up the steps to the podium—*how tall and grownup she'd gotten in the four years of caring for Annie*, I thought. Olivia adjusted the microphone up and surveyed the hundreds of friends and family up in the balcony and seated in front of her on the main floor. She didn't seem nervous at all. She had seen the gates of hell attack her little sister. She witnessed Annie's last breath. But her young faith was not in what she'd seen. It was in the unseen reality of a God who raises the dead. "If God *is* for us, who *can be* against us? Neither death nor life…nor any other created thing will separate us from the love of God in Christ Jesus our Lord." *(Romans 8:31,38,39)*

Bill stood to give Annie's eulogy, dressed in a dark suit with a pink tie, identical to the pink ties our five sons wore that day. "Annie's hope isn't that she was a cute little girl," he began. "Her hope, and ours, is that Jesus Christ died and rose again to save us from our sins so that when we die, our last breath on earth is followed by our first breath in heaven."

Bill looked tired, but his voice was steady. *Fathers aren't supposed to give their little girl's eulogies,* I thought as I looked up at him. *The vow I made to God when Bill was sick wasn't supposed to go down like this,* I thought, *that Annie would be a living testimony of God's power to heal.* Or was it, and I was just slow of heart to believe and say to God, "Not my will, but Thine be done?" Was His plan all along that Annie would be a living testimony that God not only heals on earth but in heaven too? If all the days planned for her were written in His book before she was one day old, was this His plan from the beginning?

Bill finished and walked down from the stage and sat by me, while the band played *Be Thou My Vision.* How soothing the music was to my broken heart. I closed my eyes and listened to the lyrics of the ancient 8th century hymn:

> *High King of heaven, my victory won,*
> *May I reach heaven's joys, O bright heaven's Sun!*
> *Heart of my own heart, whatever befall,*
> *Still be my Vision, O Ruler of all.*

They closed service with a song written by another bereaved father from the 19th century, *It is Well With My Soul.* The author knew sorrows like sea billows rolling over him. He knew. *Lord, haste the day when my faith shall be sight, and I see Annie again,* I thought. There's a reason hymns bring solace to those who mourn. They describe the truth of God's Word that lifts our eyes off our present circumstances and onto the reality of our future in heaven.

At the conclusion of the service Bill and our sons Taylor, Peter, Andy, David and Jack stood up and gathered around Annie's casket, faces somber and arms strong. They silently lifted her and walked out of the church to the white hearse waiting outside.

Pastor Steve prayed, then directed everyone to either go upstairs to the reception, or downstairs to visit with Bill and me. The smart people went upstairs first and found a banquet that stretched the entire length of the long hallway. Pink and white bouquets interspersed the tiers of frosted pink cupcakes, platters were stacked high with sandwiches, and punch bowls brimmed with pink lemonade. Off the hallway was a dining area with chevroned rows of white linen-covered tables, and in the center of each table, white buckets filled with pink and white tulips.

Downstairs, the receiving line stretched around the corner and wrapped around two hallways. Bill and I smiled, cried and hugged our way through hundreds of teary-eyed friends and family. "We don't know what to say," many of them whispered. *Of course not. There are no words,* I thought. It did not matter. Sometimes the best thing to say is nothing at all. Hugs and tears are eloquent enough.

After the food was eaten and most friends had filed out the front door, our family made the short trek to the cemetery across the street. The sky was gray above the green awning that sheltered ten rows of chairs, with a few blankets laid out to protect against the early spring chill. I motioned Bill's parents to come up front, and sat beside his mother, enclosing her frail 86-year-old hand in mine. Bill's mother, affectionately known as Grandmommie, had lost an infant daughter at birth. She never talked much about it, except to say that her husband, G.W., had made all the arrangements. I wondered how many poignant memories she was reliving from sixty-five years before.

Bill stood to read from the book of Psalms, and just as he opened his Bible, a ray of sun broke through the clouds and rested on our gathering. "See, God's here," my brother-in-law Dennis whispered from behind us. It was as if for a moment God held back the veil of heaven so Annie could peek down from above.

After Bill finished reading, he prayed, sat down, and two men from the mortuary staff walked forward and stood at either end of the casket. The funeral director had asked us that morning if we wanted them to lower the casket into the ground while we were there, or later after everyone was gone. Not wanting to whitewash the whole death, dying and burial process, our plan was that after they lowered the casket, everyone would pass by, drop flowers onto Annie's casket and then leave.

Some people don't like to be around when they put the casket into the ground. None of that bothered me. In my mind, Annie was dead, we had a funeral service, and now they were putting her into the ground. Everything was going pretty much according to the plan. Except for the two guys standing there waiting to lower the casket. They froze, looked down, and then back up at the mortuary director as if waiting for further instructions. She gulped, then walked over and whispered into my ear, "The casket is turned the wrong way—we need to turn it around."

There's a top and a bottom? I wondered almost aloud. *The casket is going in the ground! Who's gonna know if it's turned the wrong way?* I thought.

"Well, that's okay. If you need to turn it around, that's fine," I assured her.

Relieved, she motioned to the men. But just then, Peter stepped forward, and with Taylor, Andy, David, Jack, and Bill, they gathered around Annie's casket, lifted it, and turned it around until it was pointed the right way.

PART 3:

INTERPRETING THE STORY

Chapter 41:

GRIEF

Grief. Sadly, our culture lacks a context for it. After a loss, sometimes friends might ask us six months or a year later, "Why are you still sad?" Then we may wonder, *Well, why am I still sad?* For those who've never suffered a significant loss, it seems a logical question. But to ask that question, "Why are you still sad?" is to reveal a lack of experience with loss. In our instant gratification culture, we can sense a pressure, either from within ourselves or from others, to feel better *right now*.

"Why are you still sad?" The question itself causes us to wonder if something is wrong with us. Yet the problem isn't with those who grieve. It's with our culture that doesn't mourn very well. Margaret Mead, the noted American anthropologist, once said, "When a person is born, we rejoice, when they're married we jubilate, but when they die we try to pretend nothing happened." Sad feelings are to be covered up, avoided, glossed over. If you are sad for any extended period of time (which is to be expected in the case of the loss of someone close to you), often you're assumed to be clinically depressed, most decidedly in need of antidepressants to make it all go away.

Should grief be classified as a mental illness? This question came up the year after Annie died, when *The Lancet*, a highly regarded medical journal, took issue with the American Psychiatric Association in its fifth edition of the *Diagnostic and Statistical Manual of Mental Disorders*, or DSM. "Previous DSM editions had highlighted the need to consider, and usually exclude, bereavement before diagnosis of a major depressive disorder. In the draft version of DSM-5, however, there was no such exclusion for bereavement, which meant that feelings of deep sadness, loss, sleeplessness, crying, inability to concentrate, tiredness, and no appetite, that continue for more than two weeks after the death of a loved one could be diagnosed as depression, rather than as a normal grief reaction. The Lancet went on to say that doctors, instead of prescribing antidepressants for grief, would do better to offer time, compassion, remembrance, and empathy, than pills."[36]

Grief, with its attendant painful feelings listed in the previous paragraph, is *normal*. Our culture's expectation that people should just "snap out of it" is unreasonable. Even in 19th century Victorian England, which was known for encouraging people to keep a stiff upper lip and stuff all emotion, widows typically wore black for an entire year, with an option to renew for four. Some wore black for the remainder of their lives. There was an acceptance that grief takes time, and that outward indicators of grief, such as dark clothing, are helpful social cues for others to take greater care of those who had suffered loss. Why is that not the case today?

What cultural signals—dress, decoration, hats, scarves, pins, neon signs—do we have in our culture to signify that we are in mourning? Few, if any. Often people do their level best to hide from death and avoid discussions about funerals, mortuaries, burials, or any evidence reminding us of the brevity of life and the cold reality of death. It's as if keeping death at arm's length will keep it from touching us!

---

36   https://www.thelancet.com/journals/lancet/article/PIIS0140-6736(12)60248-7/fulltext.

"Have a good day," the checkout clerk says at the grocery store. Well, what if you're *not* having a good day? What if the little blond girl you just saw in Aisle 2 looks just like your daughter who just died? Grief in our society can be invisible and is often borne in isolation because we lack any visual or social cues to communicate a loss that words cannot describe. I often wonder if our culture's habit of grieving in isolation might actually be the root of unresolved grief or grief that extends for years. Our societal pressure to be cheerful and "suck it up" doesn't help anyone process, let alone go through, grief. In fact, stuffing the pain of loss pushes it underground where it festers, often exploding into anger, eating disorders, or substance abuse.

Instead of wearing a mask of false bravado, grievers should be given space and time to feel sadness and to cry without fear of what others may think. There's a time to weep and a time to mourn, Ecclesiastes 3:4 tells us. We need to give unashamed weeping its due time, and figure that it will be a lot longer than one might expect.

When my mother died, my more intense grief lasted about 18 months, although of course, I still have moments of missing her even thirty plus years later. After we lost Annie, it wasn't until the second year that I could think of her without crying. Even now, the glimpse of a flaxen-haired girl holding her doll and skipping along beside her mother as they cross the street can melt me into a puddle. At Starbucks recently, Bill and I stood behind a little blond girl in line ahead of us chatting it up with her mother. I looked up at the blackboard menu hanging above the cashier so that the tears would slide back into my eyes.

Inevitably after a loss, there are friends you bump into who haven't heard The.Bad.News. In a micro-second you weigh the decision of telling them with the attendant risk of—oh, the shame of it—*public emotion*—so maybe you decide to steer the conversation toward the weather. The weather is safe; your news, unfortunately, is not. The bottom line, though, is you can't always control where the news is delivered even if it's in the middle of the grocery store.

A few months after Annie died, I turned the corner with my shopping cart and saw my old friend, Jody. She was looking at greeting cards hanging in a kiosk in the center of the main walkway with her 8-year-old, daughter, Zoe. Jody and her husband moved to Oklahoma when Annie was three, and we hadn't stayed in touch. Before she moved, we used to swap babysitting; I'd take Annie over to play with Zoe while I ran errands, and she'd bring Zoe over to our place so she could do the same. Oddly, I had recently run across a picture of Zoe and Annie and regretted not keeping in touch with Jody and her family. Now here she was standing right in front of me at the grocery store. And she didn't know that Annie had died.

"Hey Jean!"

"Jody—so good to see you! Are you back in town?"

"Yeah, we moved back about four weeks ago. How is everyone?"

"We're good..."

"So everyone's well?"

"Well, no ... Annie had a brain injury about four years ago."

"WHAT?? *What? What happened?!*"

"She had a brain injury from undiagnosed Addison's disease."

"I've heard of that ... I am so sorry, Jean. I am so sorry!" Jody's eyes winced in pain.

I braced myself. I felt almost cruel for what I knew would happen next. Jody loved Annie, and my news would crush her.

"It gets worse."

"What, *what?*"

"She died ... Annie died in March."

"Oh Jean! I am in shock. I-I can't believe this. *I am so, so sorry!*" Jody dissolved into tears, and we hugged and cried right there in the middle of the aisle.

Zoe peeked from behind the kiosk and asked, "Mommy, why are you crying?"

It was painful for me to look at Zoe and not think of Annie. Annie would have been her size...*talking just like her*, I thought.

A few weeks later, I dug around in Annie's stash of stuffed toys and chose a teddy bear for Zoe to have as a remembrance of her little friend. Jody told me later that she overheard Zoe and her little sister, Braelyn, (who looks way too much like Annie), playing in their bedroom one day.

"Annie is in heaven now," Zoe explained to Braelyn, as she put Annie's teddy bear on the pillow of her bed, "and she wanted me to have her bear."

Annie's death rippled into the lives of so many people who knew her—and now mourn her. I'm glad I didn't opt for sticking with the weather in the middle of the grocery store that day. Sharing grief should not be a social faux pas. It isn't a social faux pas. It is a gift.

Chapter 42:

ASSURANCE

My supreme comfort is knowing that Annie's in heaven, and I'll see her again. Death, grief and loss are unbearable without hope. Yet after Annie died, I had doubts. I struggled with fear that maybe Annie wasn't in heaven. And how does anyone know for sure with a child who didn't demonstrate a lifetime of faith?

Years ago, when Bill was sick, I looked out onto the rows of gravestones indented in the lawn, where my friend's baby was buried. I imagined that her loss, the loss of any child, would be harder to bear than that of an adult. Now I was living in that pain. The natural order of caring for Annie was cut off. My instinct to protect her was now denied. As a Christian, everything I said I believed was being tested. Would I trust that God was taking care of her? I wanted to know—I wanted some kind of assurance she was okay. And short of having an email or text from God saying, "Yeah, I've got her, she's fine," how would I know for sure?

From all I knew of the Lord, I had to trust that He had chosen Annie even before I made the vow to have her, the vow that if God would heal Bill, we'd have a baby as a living testimony that God heals. That vow began to have new meaning to me. And although she wasn't a living testimony on earth now, I believed she was alive in heaven. Because the same God who heals on earth is the God who heals in heaven.

But one night, I needed God's comfort, not a treatise on election and predestination. Climbing the stairs on my way to bed, I begged Him for some confirmation that Annie was okay, and that she was with Him. *"Lord, just tell me she's okay. Tell me she's with you, and that she's okay."* I walked down the darkened hallway past Annie's door and into my room, sat down on the edge of my bed and checked my phone. There was an email from my sister, Rebecca. I opened it and read:

I am standing upon the seashore. A ship, at my side, spreads her white sails to the moving breeze and starts for the blue ocean. She is an object of beauty and strength. I stand and watch her until, at length, she hangs like a speck of white cloud just where the sea and sky come to mingle with each other. Then, someone at my side says, "There, she is gone."

Gone where?

Gone from my sight. That is all. She is just as large in mast, hull and spar as she was when she left my side. And, she is just as able to bear her load of living freight to her destined port. Her diminished size is in me – not in her. And, just at the moment when someone says,

"There, she is gone,"_there are other eyes watching her coming, and other voices

ready to take up the glad shout,

"Here she comes!"...and that is dying.

—*Gone From My Sight*, Rev. Luther F. Beecher

I fell to my knees, buried my face in my hands and cried, "Thank you, thank you, thank you, Jesus that Annie's with you. And thank you that Mom and Susan saw her coming and were there to greet her."

A few days later, yet another instance of comfort came to me when a friend of mine overheard a conversation between her two little girls. The Monday after Annie died, my friend, Brenda, was driving to a dentist appointment with her daughters, 6-year-old Ella (Annie's friend before her brain injury) and her 3-year-old sister, Katya. Brenda recounted their conversation in an e-mail to me later that day:

Jean—

My heart is breaking for you and your family. It is amazing how God works. He has been bringing you all to mind so much. In fact, I was praying for you all this morning in the shower. Then later this morning, the girls and I were in the car on the way to the dentist and Katya started saying, "Annie, Annie, Annie."

Then Ella said, "We know an Annie. Mom, do you know where she is?"

Katya said, "She is in heaven."

I said, "No, she is probably at home or at school." Then Ella said, "Maybe she is in the hospital." She asked if I had your number and said I should call you RIGHT THEN. Of course, I said, "No," but I would call you later.

You see I had no idea that Annie had passed on to heaven on Friday. I am so sorry for your loss. We will all miss Annie.

I am here in prayer always and please let me know how else I can support you and your family.

I love you guys,

Brenda

Comforting assurances that Annie was safe with Jesus lifted the weight of grief from me and gave me hope.

Chapter 43:

A NEW NORMAL

My body ached for three months after Annie died. At first, I thought I was sick with some sort of flu; grief often manifests through physical symptoms like aches and pains, or fatigue. By the time I'd gone through a bottle of Advil over the span of a few weeks, it occurred to me that the pain in my body mirrored the pain in my heart.

Not surprisingly, Bill and I grieved differently. Men and women often do. I also had a bit of an unfair advantage—if you can call it that—because I had experienced the deaths of my mother and my sister and had more of a grief roadmap than he did. I knew that it's typical for a person suffering loss to:

1. Be excruciatingly sad to the point that they can't breathe for about three to six months

2. Come up for air around six months and then be sad for another six months

3. Go through another year of adjustment, with days or weeks of normalcy thrown in

In contrast, after Annie died Bill thought that in about three months he should feel back to normal again and was surprised when that didn't happen. He shared recently with me that he was glad I was there to hold the flashlight up for him through those dark days and didn't belittle him for his unrealistic expectations.

After she died, one of the more difficult situations for Bill was Sunday mornings at church. His routine when the service was almost over was to pick up Annie from her class and then wheel her into the sanctuary, lift her out of her wheelchair and hold her in his lap while the last few songs were sung. Now after the service, the tears just rolled down his cheeks, for there was no longer a little girl to retrieve from the children's ministry rooms and no little girl to hold on his lap.

After she died, we grieved two Annies. Although we'd already spent four years mourning the healthy Annie we'd lost after the brain injury, now we missed the Annie in her wheelchair. The sadness after her death seemed to be a continuation of the four years of grief we'd already endured. There was an odd sense of comfort, though, to realize that we had bonded so strongly with that little Tinker Bell in the purple wheelchair. There were so many facets to her personality, and we missed them all.

My friends gathered around me in the months after she died, and many reached out with invitations to go out and grab some coffee. At first, I tried to keep up with them all; I appreciated their empathy and at the time I felt that going out for coffee would be a good way to process. After a while, though, I found more of a need to be alone with my thoughts. The physical weight of grief forced me to slow down. Grieving seemed to develop a rhythm: steady, unhurried, plodding. Solitude replaced social engagements. Being alone wasn't something I feared or disliked but evolved into a safe sanctuary of sorts. On the other hand, I also wanted to talk about Annie to anyone who would listen! I didn't want anyone to forget that she was...just *here*. The need to talk about Annie took precedence over any social conventions of "don't ask, don't tell" about your loss, your grief. I wanted to repeat her name. Out loud. *Annie. Annie. Annie.*

I began to recognize the glazed look in people's eyes when I'd talk of my daughter who had just died. So, I'd censor myself—most of the time. Occasionally, though, I'd jump in with both feet, sometimes with Bill or the kids cringing beside me.

Shortly after Annie died, we all sat down at a restaurant, and the server introduced herself: "Hi, I'm Brittany, I'll be taking care of you tonight. Are y'all out celebrating a special occasion?"

"Ah, yes, we just placed the headstone on my daughter's grave," I said matter-of-factly.

Brittany took one step backward. My kids' eyes bored holes into their napkins. *"Really,* Mom? Did you have to say that?" I'm sure they were thinking.

Or at the florist: "Who are these pretty pink flowers for?"

"I'm actually placing them on my daughter's grave."

"Oh, I'm so sorry."

"No, it's okay."

"How old was she?"

"Almost eight."

"Ohhh." Tears from the clerk provoked tears from me. Rats. *Maybe next time the pink flowers will be for no special reason,* I thought to myself. Or... maybe shedding tears in public is okay.

We created a place to mourn Annie. Everyone who suffers a loss decides what works for them: cremation, traditional in-ground burial, mausoleum, spreading the ashes or keeping them in an urn. We chose a traditional burial for Annie in a cemetery so that her five brothers and sister could visit there whenever they wanted. They loved Annie and having a place to go was one way to provide them with a physical place to grieve and a place to remember.

They still stop by occasionally, and sometimes I find bouquets of flowers left at her grave for their little sister who is still missed so much.

When I visit her grave, I often wonder what it will be like when Jesus comes again. The Bible says that the dead in Christ will rise first.[37] And honestly, I want to see Annie rising out of her grave, good as new. I want to be the first to hug her again. I don't know if God will grant me that request. But I hope He does.

Of course, the first year was hard for all of us, especially the first holidays. Driving to the grocery store with Jack that November, he confided to me that he'd been to the Disney store at the mall earlier that week. Each year before Annie died, Jack bought a stuffed toy for her there: an orangutan, a monkey, or whatever, and gave it to her for Christmas. But that first year he walked into the store and thought, *No reason to buy a toy for Annie this year.* Still, he was drawn inside, "just to look." As he thought of the little sister who no longer waits at home for a toy, he wiped his eyes and hurried out before anyone could see the tears running down his cheeks. "I hope my first child is a girl. It's a blessing to be able to pamper a little girl," he said quietly.

After Annie died, Olivia told me one day that she wished she could "move on" in her grief, but kept having dreams of Annie almost every night that seemed to pull her back into an overwhelming sense of sadness. In her dream the night before, Olivia said she was holding Annie very tightly, which Annie was resisting as she always would, but Olivia just didn't want to let her go. When Olivia woke up, she said she just wanted to go right back to sleep, and back to her dream so she could hold Annie one more time.

Annie was Olivia's little shadow for her first three and a half years, following her around the house, squirming while Olivia fixed her hair; sometimes she was a pest, sometimes she was a hoot. And when Annie had her brain injury Olivia was often the first in line (by desire or default) to help me with caregiving. Olivia often shared her bed with Annie in the early morning

---

37   1 Thessalonians 4:16.

hours on the weekends, she went with us to doctor appointments, and she attended to Annie's most basic needs. So, when Annie died, it shouldn't have surprised me when Olivia said she felt her purpose in life had been buried with her little sister.

I tried to help Olivia see a bigger reality, that our hope and comfort was knowing Annie was in heaven. But my understanding and acceptance of Annie's death didn't automatically transfer to Olivia. Maybe I was too close, maybe I wasn't reading her clues carefully—but what I was saying simply wasn't making sense to her. Nothing I said or did seemed to help her climb out of her despair. I took her to counseling, something we should have done from the beginning. But even counseling has its limitations. Sometimes God just needs to speak to us, reassure us, comfort us, in a way only He can do.

Olivia and I were already running late for a counseling appointment one brisk fall October afternoon. As we rushed to get there, I thought it ironic that the road to her appointment ran alongside the cemetery where Annie is buried. As we approached the stoplight at the intersection, I glanced over and caught sight of a spectacular rainbow suspended against the dark sky. It was a perfect arc, both ends visible, with the top peaking right over Annie's grave. I glanced at my watch—only a few minutes to spare—then impulsively pulled into the drive of the cemetery to get a better look.

"Mom, what are you doing? We're late," Olivia protested.

"This'll only take a minute...we need to look at this...this is a-maz..."

The luminous red, orange, yellow, green, blue and violet colors stretched from one end of the cemetery to the other. We sat there as long as we dared, figuring that being forgivably late was of secondary importance to being providentially on time to witness this brilliant banner lighting up the dark clouds, standing watch over Annie's grave. Was God drawing our eyes up above her grave and what we had lost and onto Him? Annie's life is hidden in Christ, especially now, to us. The rainbow reminded us of the radiance surrounding the heavenly throne Annie sees now. And someday we will see it, and her, too.

And He who sat there was like a jasper and sardius stone in appearance; And *there was* a rainbow around the throne, in appearance like an emerald.

Revelation 4:3

Chapter 44:

SORTING THROUGH

Eventually we needed to decide what to do with Annie's bedroom. One of my sons wanted us to leave everything enshrined as-is. Don't touch anything, leave it the way it was when Annie died. But another sibling was hoping to move into her more spacious room. So, a compromise was in order.

Pragmatic me just wanted to pack up most of Annie's things and put them away, leaving a few keepsakes around the house to remember her by. Plus, just as we had with Bill, I wanted to scour the house of all the medical paraphernalia we had accumulated over four years. Diapers, wipes, medication cups, syringes, cans of food, food bags, medicine, and those hideous pink throw up bins—I wanted it all gone. All the reminders of my little sick Annie, and the suffering she endured, needed to be purged. Yet, my desire to clear it away had to be tempered with the needs of those whose grief process was slower and not inclined to rash sweeps. Neither way of mourning is wrong, but I needed to be gentle in my approach.

Maybe if they had Annie mementos in their rooms, cleaning up her stuff won't seem so abrupt, I thought. So, one blanket and one stuffed toy of hers found their way onto each of my kid's rooms, along with photo collages I made of each sibling with Annie over the years. I wanted the pictures to be comforting evidence of their love and care of Annie.

"Guilt is perhaps the most painful companion of death," Elizabeth Kubler-Ross wrote, and this was probably the case for many in our family. A few of our children said that they struggled with guilt, feeling like they were not patient enough with Annie. The fact was, caring for Annie was intense. Eyes on her at all times, grabbing those pink plastic bins to catch her sudden gastrointestinal explosions, unexpected seizures—it pushed us all to the limits of our ability to cope. They all, we all, did the best we could. Now, I thought, should be a time for remembering the good. Photos, favorite blankets, and familiar toys were all good things to remember Annie by.

While I was slogging through all of Annie's stuff, my friend Maurita called and offered to help.

"Jean? How are you doing?"

"Hi, Maurita. Okay, I guess."

"You know, I was thinking. I don't know when you might want to do this... no rush... but if you need help going through Annie's stuff, I could do that," she said.

The paper crafting she did for Annie's memorial displays was only the tip of Maurita's many gifts. She also takes organization to new levels. She came over one morning and sorted Annie's belongings into three categories: save, give away, and throw out. If I couldn't decide which pile to put something, Maurita would just set it aside until I could make a decision. And, at Maurita's suggestion, we took a picture of anything I wanted to give away, so that at least the photo would be something to hold on to.

Annie's pink jacket, most of her hair bows, and the glittery dresses her Aunt Susie bought each Christmas were saved. Annie's high-tech activity chair went to little friend, Nale, her comrade at church who also uses wheels to get around. Annie's school artwork went into a keepsake box. Her wheelchair went to a child in need within the school district. Her leg braces and shoes and food backpack went into the attic. I don't know why I saved the food backpack; I just couldn't throw it away.

About halfway through our sorting marathon, it occurred to me that some of Annie's belongings could go to the children who knew her, giving them a measure of comfort. After all, their young hearts were mourning, too. So, many of Annie's outfits went to her classroom buddies at school. Two of her favorite stuffed toys went to her cousins, Grace and Aileen. And Annie's treasure chest of princess <u>Cinderellella</u> dress-up clothes went to Maurita's daughter, Maddie, who danced around in them the whole time we sifted through Annie's stuff.

Chapter 45:

LITTLE CHILDREN GRIEVE TOO

Before Annie's brain injury, Grace and Aileen, my niece Lorraine's twin girls, used to swing in the backyard with Annie, all of them singing "Kumbaya" at the top of their lungs. They were only 10 years old when Annie died and struggled like the rest of us with her passing. Lorraine sent me this email that Thanksgiving.

"I was thinking of all the reasons why I'm thankful and last Sunday at church we had a service where anyone could come up to say why we are thankful as well. After a few families shared what they're thankful for, Grace and Aileen cajoled their friends to come up with them to give thanks. Aileen stammered and then said she was thankful that Annie was in heaven and could eat. I just couldn't look up after that. Kleenex in hand, I was a mess. Needless to say, she said what was in my heart. I miss her, I miss all of you and I'm glad she's well again."

After reading Lorraine's email I was a mess, too. What sweet comfort that Grace and Aileen carry Annie so close to their hearts! They prayed fervently through the years of Annie's illness, begging God to heal their little cousin. And now, without minimizing their loss of Annie, their faith was big enough to thank God that today Annie is well again and can eat!

The grief of a child is real, and each child feels and expresses it differently. Carolyn, one of Annie's friends in her Life skills class at school is nonverbal. Nonverbal doesn't equate to non-communicative, however. Her mother shared with me that their teacher "has a series of videos on her iPhone of the kids, and one of them is of Annie. She said Carolyn loves to choose that one to watch, and kisses the screen while she watches it. We never know with her just what she is taking in and what things have impacted her. It's obvious, though, that she remembers her friend." Words aren't necessary for Carolyn to express what is in her heart.

The spring after Annie died, her classmates, paraeducators and staff all gathered in front of the school to plant a garden in Annie's memory. Her teacher took lots of pictures while the children dug in the dirt planting a weeping cherry tree along with a profusion of pink, white and purple shrubs and flowers. The garden was a tangible way for the staff at Annie's school to help her little friends (and themselves!) express their grief. At the end of the school year, they invited me to the dedication of the garden. As I looked around at all the faces of the children and the discrete dabbing of the eyes of the school staff, it was clear that there still was a big Annie-sized hole in their hearts. Knowing that my burden of grief was shared with her friends, as well as the entire community of people who taught her, cared for her, prayed for her, and loved her made it lighter to bear.

Chapter 46:

TIME

After Annie died I had time. Time that had been devoted to caring for Annie was now empty and not yet filled with...anything. Being able to slow down was a gift, however, and gave me time to think, remember, and bake cookies.

Before Annie's brain injury, she used to help me in the kitchen, but after she got sick I didn't cook much at all. From the day of her brain injury, my time revolved around keeping Annie alive, which meant meals became fast, boxed, or takeout. Preparing food took time and attention, neither of which I had much of, especially for something as nonessential as cookies.

Time also revolved around Annie's feeding schedule which was three times a day, for two and a half hours at a time, and slowly all night long because she didn't have the stomach capacity for anything more. And because she couldn't tell us when she felt full, we'd often see what went down a second time. I guess you could say that cookies *were* a part of that scenario.

The first Christmas after she died, I stood in our kitchen one evening listening to Christmas music, making cut-out cookies and missing my little helper, wishing she were there again opening and closing that silly pantry door. My thoughts drifted back to the last Christmas Annie helped me bake cookies, and as I reminisced I had a dream, or maybe it was a vision, or just a thought:

The Man and the little girl watched the woman roll out the sugar cookie dough and carefully cut out the trees, bells and stars. The little girl remembered the stars—she loved watching the stars at night. The Man often told her how much the woman thought of her and missed her.

"Can You tell her that I miss her, too?" she asked Him.

The woman continued rolling the dough and cutting out the cookies. Soft music floated in from the living room while the woman worked with the dough, her memory filling in the words of the music:

For the beauty of the earth, for the glory of the skies, for the love which from our birth over and around us lies;

Lord of all, to thee we raise this our hymn of grateful praise.

F.S. Pierpoint, *For the Beauty of the Earth.*

The little girl tugged at His robe and persisted. "And if you told her I miss her, how would I know if she really heard?"

The woman's thoughts drifted back to the last time she made Christmas cut-out cookies, so long ago. She had a little helper then, who liked to mix the dough and lick the spoon.

For the joy of human love,
brother sister, parent, child,
friends on earth and friends above,
for all gentle thoughts and mild;
Lord of all, to thee we raise t
his our hymn of grateful praise.

The little girl continued to watch from above as the woman cut out another star and hummed along to the music coming from the next room. The woman suddenly recalled how her little helper used to sing that song— part of a children's collection of hymns. It had been one of her favorites, one she always would half-sing, half-yell, "Lord of all to thee we raise, this our hymn of grateful praise!"

The woman's eyes stung as she placed the next star on the cookie sheet.

The Man leaned down to the little girl and whispered in her ear, "Do you wonder how you'll know if she really heard you?"

They watched silently as the woman brushed a tear away with her flour-smudged hand.

"That's how," He said, as He held the little girl close to His side.

For thyself, best Gift Divine,
to the world so freely given,
peace on earth, and joy in heaven:
Lord of all, to thee we raise
this our hymn of grateful praise.

Chapter 47:

AUTOPSY

We wanted to know, if we *could* know, why Annie had Addison's disease, how it affected her organs, and anything else about what went on inside her body that caused the effects we could see outside her body. We already knew from MRIs in 2007 that her brain was severely compromised. But if we could learn anything else we wanted to know. So, we signed the papers for an autopsy.

The results came back in May and showed that Annie's adrenal glands were very small, but the appearance of them didn't fit into any known subtypes of congenital adrenal hyperplasia (CAH). When Annie was a newborn she tested negative for CAH. We also knew from previous blood tests that she had no adrenal antibodies that would indicate an autoimmune issue, which is often the cause of Addison's disease. Simply put, there were no obvious conclusions as to why Annie's adrenal glands didn't work. Most of her doctors referred to her condition as Addison's. But it may have been a rare type of CAH. We just don't know.

The only notable finding was in Annie's pancreas. What should have been normal pancreatic tissue was replaced with fat. A normal pancreas produces hormones necessary for digestion, but since Annie's was mostly fat it didn't produce enough, if any, of those hormones. Annie's defective pancreas wasn't a result of the brain injury, nor was it cumulative damage from all the drugs she was on. The autopsy reported that it was fatty *before* her brain injury, indicating a congenital, or birth, defect.

This helped to explain why Annie was thin from toddlerhood on, and why she continued having trouble gaining weight after the brain injury. If her damaged pancreas had absorption issues, this also would explain why she needed more hydrocortisone than any other kid her size and weight. It was likely that the hydrocortisone she did get wasn't absorbed properly, and that's the reason she needed more hydrocortisone, or should have gotten hydrocortisone intramuscularly. What was disconcerting to us was that this problem with her pancreas was noted in an abdominal MRI right after her brain injury, but for some reason the information was never passed along.

For four years we fed Annie via a G-tube, and both her doctors and we often wondered why she couldn't gain weight. During Annie's final hospitalization when the flu completely shut down her gut, the doctors put her on TPN, or total parenteral nutrition. TPN switched the "on" button for Annie—her eyes lit up, she babbled constantly, she took walks around the hospital in her Kidwalk, and her pale, sallow skin turned a healthy pink. It was an amazing transformation, all because the TPN didn't require pancreatic hormones, it just fed Annie through her veins. But at that point, no one knew her pancreas didn't work; the information from her 2007 post-brain injury abdominal MRI must have been sitting in a file somewhere.

People on TPN are at great risk for IV site infections, so after being on TPN for about a week in March of 2011, the plan was for Annie to go back to tube feeding through her stomach, a much safer feeding alternative. Safer maybe, but for her, not effective at all. Her doctor and I discussed this in the week before she died. We agreed to try one more time to get her GJ-tube feeds up to a fast enough rate for her to get the amount per day she needed. If that didn't work, a permanent TPN central line would be placed. Before any of that happened, though, Annie developed the urinary tract infection that morphed into sepsis, and she died.

When I ruminate about these things, I force myself to remember what I know is true: God planned the number of Annie's days. Every one of them. How many times did I sit with Annie reading that book, *What Does God Do?*, where it quotes Psalm 139:16, "All the days planned for me were written in Your book before I was one day old." It's not coincidental that I read that book to her. God knew the time would come when *I* needed to cling to the truth of that verse.

I'm not saying that we, or medical providers, aren't responsible for the decisions we make. We all are, and we bear a variety of consequences for those decisions. But over each and every decision: good, bad, indifferent, wise, or unwise, God is sovereign. *He* determined the number of Annie's days.

C h a p t e r   4 8 :

LOSS THROUGH THE
LENS OF ETERNITY

fter Annie died and the intensity of caring for her was lifted, I saw more clearly the similarities between Bill's disease and Annie's, in fact, their illnesses closely mirrored one another's. Bill had balance problems as did Annie. Bill couldn't eat without choking and neither could Annie. Bill had a disabled parking permit, so did Annie. Bill needed a cane, Annie needed a wheelchair. Bill had trouble thinking and processing information, Annie lost her bright mind, too. But the most tragically ironic twist of their stories is that Bill was healed overnight, and Annie became severely disabled overnight. Why? Why did all of this happen to one family, to *us?* Why did Annie's and Bill's illnesses so closely parallel each other, and what are we to make of why it happened?

As I mentioned before, we are all meaning-makers, and desire to frame our life experiences in a narrative that helps us understand *why?* If I think, *Bill got sick for three years and then God healed him miraculously, overnight, in response to the prayers of many,* I've just interpreted that 1) God healed him miraculously; it wasn't a fluke, and 2) it was in response to prayer. I've interpreted from the facts of Bill's sudden recovery that I believe what God says in the Bible: that He can heal, and that often healing is in response to prayer.[38]

When Annie was born, I interpreted her birth as an answer to prayer, because I had made a promise to God. My plan was that Annie would be a living testimony to God's power to heal. But what happened is that she suffered a catastrophic brain injury, lived with severe disability for four years, and then died.

Over all the facts are interpretations of those facts. But rather than sink in despair about losing Annie, I desperately wanted to see it through an eternal, or timeless, viewpoint. Not that an eternal perspective would magically erase my grief, but it would give her death meaning. Of course, as much as we all try, some things are mysteries that we will never understand this side of heaven. But seven truths helped me make some sense of what happened:

1. God decides how long we live. The Bible says He sovereignly determines the number of our days. That's one reason we chose Psalm 139:16 for Annie's headstone, "All the days planned for me were written in Your book before I was one day old." My acceptance of Annie's death is anchored in the fact that God decides how many days we live. Although many human factors contributed to Annie's disability and death, God was sovereign over it all.

2. God expanded our ministry to include people who grieve, specifically, parents who grieve the loss of a child. Did I want that ministry? Of course not. However, if I am bought with a price—Jesus paid for me with His life—then laying down my life and everything that is precious to me should not be a stretch. If that includes walking through the valley of the shadow of death with Annie so I can "speak the language" of others who have lost their children, then I accept that ministry. As 2 Corinthians 1:4 says, God "comforts us in all our troubles, so that we can comfort those in any trouble with the comfort we ourselves receive from God."

---

38   James 5:15.

3. God allowed Bill's and Annie's sicknesses to show His power through weakness. God loves people with disabilities. Often those with disabilities are weak or marginalized and not able to advocate for themselves. The Bible says, "He has chosen the weak things of the world to put to shame the things which are mighty."[39] Sadly, physical disability doesn't fit neatly in a world that values youth, health, and beauty. As I cared for Bill and then for Annie, I learned the blessing of identifying with the weak. Jesus took on our weakness, and I learned a little of what that means as I cared for Bill and Annie.

4. God tested and refined me through caregiving. Caregiving reveals our selfishness every day. Caring for another person is stressful, especially when every action you take, or neglect to take, has a direct bearing on the well-being of another. It is both a responsibility and burden. It's easy to get angry about it, push against it, and turn away from it, but Jesus said when we care for the least of these—whatever "least" is—we are doing it for Him.

5. God gave us Annie as a living testimony to His power to heal in heaven. This is the most important thing I learned. I could have interpreted her death as a consummate loss. The Apostle Paul directly confronted this thinking when he wrote in Philippians that "to live is Christ, and to die is gain."[40] Accordingly, I count Annie's death as "gain" because she has been made new in heaven. God's reality is that Annie *is* a living testimony to His power to heal—not on earth as He did for Bill—but in heaven. How can I argue against that? After all my prayers that Annie would be healed, why should I complain now? She *is* healed! Do I still miss Annie and grieve her daily? Of course. And each member of our family does. But my overarching thought and comfort is that she is healed today, and I will see her again very soon.

---

39   1 Corinthians 1:27.

40   Philippians 1:21.

6. How we interpret the events of our lives drives us either closer to God or away from Him. The same event can happen to two different people and produce two different responses. As believers in Jesus, our attitudes toward suffering should reflect the truth of God's Word that suffering is *normative* here on earth and not a sign God doesn't love us, isn't near or doesn't care. Our mindset should be that He will sustain us in our suffering here on earth, and deliver us through it, or deliver us out of it and into heaven.

7. How we interpret pain, suffering and loss in our lives either points people to Jesus or away from Him. By focusing on ourselves, our loss, our disappointment, and our anger, we tell the world our hope is firmly planted on earth. However, by seeing our pain, suffering or loss through an eternal lens, we extract meaning and purpose out of it, and in turn, are able to point others to an eternal reality. This isn't a Pollyanna mentality but an understanding that although tragedy happens, there are divine purposes at work as well. Seeing the good doesn't erase the bad, but it does give it meaning.

Again, we see this in the Old Testament story of Joseph, who was sold into slavery by his brothers, imprisoned for a decade, and brought up out of his dungeon to serve as second in command in Egypt. From his new position, he administered the food supply during a seven-year drought. And who came to him for food? His brothers. Instead of bewailing the misery God had allowed in his life and perhaps exacting retribution on his brothers, he said to them, "You meant evil against me, but God meant it for good, to bring it about that many people should be kept alive, as they are today."[41] Joseph acknowledged his brothers' sin, "You meant evil against me," but understood and believed that "God meant it for good."

I questioned why God would allow Annie to get sick in the middle of the night when we couldn't help her. I questioned why no doctor diagnosed her before her brain injury. These are facts. But I can't just interpret the facts

---

41   Genesis 50:20.

from an earthly perspective. I need to see them through God's eyes, and His eternal viewpoint. A biblical view of suffering and loss is the linchpin to interpreting the suffering we go through. I still don't know all of what God wants to accomplish from our story. I probably never will. But what I do know is this: Jesus Christ is the One who makes all things new. He paid the punishment for our sin that we deserve by dying on the cross, and He rose again, conquering sin and death. He's the One who redeems our souls, as well as our losses. He's the One who helped me make sense of Bill's sickness and healing on earth, and Annie's sickness and healing in heaven.

It's not that God is callous to our grief, pain, and suffering. On the contrary, He endured all of that, to an infinitely greater degree. He has compassion as One who has suffered, even to death. As we suffer here on earth—and we will—His desire is that we put our pain in the context that it deserves:

For our light affliction, which is but for a moment,

is working for us a far more exceeding *and eternal weight of glory.*

2 Corinthians 4:17

EPILOGUE

I stared at the screen, reading on Facebook that a friend had just lost her 23-year-old son in a car accident. Lonnie and I both had large families; we used to go to dinner at her house years ago where our kids filled up at least two long tables. Her sons were friends with my sons and now she had just been initiated into this hellish sorority of mothers who have lost children.

Lonnie, as well as a few old friends from the church we'd gone to years ago had reconnected through Facebook. As I counted up all the women from that church who had lost children, the number came to nine. *Nine mothers from one church who had all lost children?* I thought...*How could this be?* Their children ranged in age from birth to school aged and into early adulthood.

How could all these friends of mine be bereaved mothers? We, who went to church together—had it been ten years since most of us had seen each other? The church where all seemed to go so well for so long, and yet from where most of us had fled? Aside from the passing years, the one barrier that kept us apart was reliving the pain from that church we'd just as soon forget.

Now it seemed the pain from losing our children might be the glue that would bring us back together. I felt God whisper, "You guys need to get together, and we can make this happen." Yet for every good reason to get together, I could think of a bad one:

Wouldn't it be great for these mothers to be able to share their loss with other women who understood?

But what if no one wants to talk about their dead children?

Wouldn't it be great for all of us to renew our friendship again from years ago?

But what if they didn't want to?

I decided to put it out there and see what came of it. The worst that could happen is they'd say no. But what if they said *yes?* A gathering like this had the potential of healing on numerous levels. So I prayed and asked God to lead the way, if indeed this was His idea.

I messaged one of the moms who had some years between her loss and the present. She would tell me if it was a good idea or a dumb one. Fortunately, she was all in.

A private Facebook page would be the conduit for everyone to connect. Most of the mothers were on Facebook already, but a couple of them needed to be invited. I called it "Mothers Who Have Lost Children." Simple enough.

Next, we needed to decide on a date close enough to generate excitement, but far enough out to allow for everyone to be there. President's Day weekend was good for everyone and gave us two months to bring all the details together. Finally, we had to find a place to gather. After floating a couple of options, I asked my friend, Pam, if we could stay at her cottage at Ocean Shores.

"Of course—I'd be honored!" she said. I knew she would. Pam and I have been friends since Bill began working at our church before Annie was born. She was the one who rocked Annie in the nursery at church and after Annie's brain injury brought me lattes at the hospital each morning at 7 a.m.

And she had worked with the neurologist who cared for Annie from the day of her brain injury to the day she died.

Pam welcomed us to meet in their home, a three-bedroom, two-bath bungalow with a big front porch on one side and a deck that looked out onto a canal on the other. It was a cozy, welcoming, and spacious retreat for all the moms to meet. Finally, everything was set. It occurred to me that we should have a loosely defined agenda to make the time focused and helpful. Okay, I'm somewhat task-oriented. Agenda driven. Whatever. We needed a direction to go in, and that was my gift.

Gifts? Perfect! What were some of the gifts of the women who would be coming? Joanie sang and led worship in our old church and could do that for us. Katie was a great cook and could rule the kitchen. So it went—everyone stepped up with a job to do and a contribution to make our time special.

President's Day weekend came quickly but unfortunately, two of our moms couldn't make it. For the seven of us who were able to go, though, an almost sacred time together was about to begin. We arrived within a half hour of each other and spent at least another hour in a mass hug-fest. Pam greeted us at the top of her porch, and we all followed her into the kitchen where the scent of cookies fresh from the oven filled the air. Gift bags personalized with each mom's name were set out on the farmhouse table. Her face glowed with the pleasure of being able to serve these women whom she knew had suffered the loss every parent fears.

Pam showed us around the house, gave us some housekeeping details, "Don't forget to turn off the ice maker when you leave!" then gave us all another hug and left. We dragged our bags in from the cars, staked out our bedrooms—snorers, early-birds and night owls grouped together—then met in the great room with drinks in hand and smiles on faces. A few guarded glances shot around. I sensed we needed to begin peeling away any anxiety anyone had brought with them. We settled into the stuffed couches and took turns tentatively recounting our child's life and what happened when they died. As we began to share the details of our individual stories, defenses came down, and our hearts were knit together in compassion and love.

When I told Bill why we were meeting at Pam's, he thought talking about our children who had died sounded like a weekend of torture. I reminded him women typically like to verbalize their pain, and that it would be cathartic. And, of course, it was. What a relief it was to talk about our children, say their names, and cry without the need to stifle thoughts or feelings or to sanitize them for the audience. No uneasy looks, no pat clichés, just an unending supply of love, tissues and time. We all took as much time as we wanted to eke out every last minute detail of our losses.

We also discussed how losing a child affected our marriages. Sadly, for a few, their child's death seemed to trigger extramarital affairs. Shortcuts around grief only compound the pain, and while two of the marriages survived the affairs, two did not. We also shared how losing a child affected the surviving siblings, as their reactions ranged from depression and anger to suicide attempts. Many surviving siblings struggled with guilt. Some still do. And as mothers, we agreed one of the on-going battles after the loss of our child is the fear of losing another child. All our stories bore out the fact that the loss of a child is like a bomb going off in our homes, creating collateral damage often as crippling as the initial loss itself.

Our conversation shifted to a happier topic when we remembered the things people did after our child died that helped us. One mother described how the firemen of the station where her husband worked never left them alone for the first month, serving their every need. Another described the frequent e-mails she got from a friend, reminding her that she was in her prayers.

Then the question, "What would you say to a mother who is newly bereaved?" ignited an explosion of chatter.

"Well, I can tell you what *not* to say. Don't say, 'Well, maybe you should get a pet.'"

"No one said that to you!"

"Yes, they did."

"How about, 'you have an angel now'? My daughter is not an angel. She's in heaven, but she's not an angel for cryin' out loud!"

We each had our pet peeves, but we agreed what was most helpful was when people drew near to us and didn't say much at all. Filling up quiet spaces with words often did not comfort but only brought more pain.

"Just tell her you're sorry for her loss. Sit with her. Bring her food. Clean her house. But don't tell her 'all things work together for good.' It might be true, but she doesn't want to hear that the day she buries her kid."

God's redemptive work was written all over that weekend in Ocean Shores. And with each year that passes since Annie's death, God continues to send His healing grace upon our family, and in the hearts of grieving parents He sends our way. It is His way to upend our expectations. To bring life from death. To redeem our losses. And to help us trust Him for each day He has planned for us.

GLOSSARY

Adrenal Insufficiency—Adrenal insufficiency is an endocrine, or hormonal, disorder that occurs when the adrenal glands do not produce enough cortisol or aldosterone, essential hormones necessary to mount a defense in times of stress or illness. The adrenal glands are located just above the kidneys. Adrenal insufficiency can be primary or secondary.

Addison's Disease—The common term for primary adrenal insufficiency, occurs when the adrenal glands are damaged and cannot produce enough of the hormone cortisol.

AFO's—The AFO (Ankle Foot Orthosis) has been used for decades to treat physical problems with the lower limb. AFO's are commonly used to treat foot drop due to Stroke, MS (Multiple Sclerosis), CP (Cerebral Palsy), Nerve Damage, Spinal Cord Injuries, Traumatic Brain Injuries, and General Weakness. http://www.orthomedics.us/Pages/ankle.aspx

ALS—Amyotrophic lateral sclerosis (ALS), often referred to as "Lou Gehrig's Disease," is a progressive neurodegenerative disease that affects nerve cells in the brain and the spinal cord. Motor neurons reach from the brain to the spinal cord and from the spinal cord to the muscles throughout the body. The progressive degeneration of the motor neurons in ALS eventually leads to death. When the motor neurons die, the ability of the brain to initiate and control muscle movement is lost. With voluntary muscle action progressively affected, patients in the later stages of the disease may become totally paralyzed. http://www.alsa.org/about-als/what-is-als.html.

Brain injury storming—Following acute multiple trauma, hypothalamic stimulation of the sympathetic nervous system and adrenal glands causes an increase in circulating corticoids and catecholamines, or a stress response. In individuals with severe traumatic brain injury or a Glasgow Coma Scale score of 3-8, this response can be exaggerated and episodic. A term commonly used by nurses caring for these individuals to describe this phenomenon is *storming*. Symptoms can include alterations in level of consciousness, increased posturing, dystonia, hypertension, hyperthermia, tachycardia, tachypnea, diaphoresis, and agitation. These individuals generally are at a low level of neurological activity with minimal alertness, minimal awareness, and reflexive motor response to stimulation, and the storming can take a seemingly peaceful individual into a state of chaos. Denise M. Lemke, Journal of Neuroscience Nursing. https://www.proquest. com/openview/23ba95ffa685a07c285be540e58b7843/1?pq-origsite=g-scholar&cbl=48278.

Bulbar symptoms—Progressive bulbar palsy, also called progressive bulbar atrophy, involves the brain stem—the bulb-shaped region containing lower motor neurons needed for swallowing, speaking, chewing, and other functions. Symptoms include pharyngeal muscle weakness (involved with swallowing), weak jaw and facial muscles, progressive loss of speech, and tongue muscle atrophy. Limb weakness with both lower and upper motor neuron signs is almost always evident but less prominent. Individuals are at increased risk of choking and aspiration pneumonia, which is caused by the passage of liquids and food through the vocal folds and into the lower airways and lungs. Affected persons have outbursts of laughing or crying (called emotional lability). http://www.ninds.nih.gov/disorders/motor_neuron_diseases/ detail_motor_neuron_diseases.htm

DIC—Disseminated intravascular coagulation (DIC) is a rare, life-threatening condition that prevents blood from clotting normally. The blood clots reduce blood flow and can block blood from reaching bodily organs. This increased clotting can use up the blood's platelets and clotting factors. Fewer platelets and clotting factors available result in excessive bleeding. http://www.healthline.com/health/disseminated-intravascular-coagulation-dic#Overview1

Emergency Injection of Solu-Cortef —In an emergency, anyone with Addison's disease can experience symptoms of extreme weakness, a serious drop in blood pressure and mental confusion. This means they need extra steroid medication immediately and may need an emergency injection. As a general rule, an Addisonian should give themselves an emergency injection of 100mg hydrocortisone sodium (Efcortesol™ or Solu-Cortef®) as soon as they vomit. This minimizes the risks of impaired gastric absorption that some people experience in the early stages of adrenal emergency (hypocortisolaemia). Giving too much steroid during injury or illness will do no harm. Under-replacement is potentially life-threatening, or may have other severe outcomes due to circulatory/cardiovascular complications from low blood pressure. http://www.addisons.org.uk/info/emergency/page3.html

Hydrocortisone—Corticosteroid medication is used to replace the hormones called cortisol and aldosterone that your body no longer produces. It is usually taken in tablet form two or three times a day. In most cases, a medication called hydrocortisone is used to replace the cortisol. http://www.nhs.uk/Conditions/Addisons-disease/Pages/Treatment.aspx

Hypoxic Brain Injury—The brain requires a constant flow of oxygen to function normally. A hypoxic-anoxic injury, also known as HAI, occurs when that flow is disrupted, essentially starving the brain, and preventing it from performing vital biochemical processes. *Hypoxic* refers to a partial lack of oxygen; *anoxic* means a total lack. In general, the more complete the deprivation, the more severe the harm to the brain and the greater the consequences. The diminished oxygen supply can cause serious impairments in cognitive skills, as well as in physical, psychological and other functions. Recovery *can* occur in many cases, but it depends largely on the parts of the brain affected, and its pace and extent are unpredictable. https://www.caregiver.org/hypoxic-anoxic-brain-injury

Intraosseous Cannulation—For patients in extremis from respiratory failure or shock, securing vascular access is crucial, along with establishing an airway and ensuring adequacy of breathing and ventilation. Peripheral intravenous catheter insertion is often difficult, if not impossible, in infants and young children with circulatory collapse. Intraosseous (IO) needle placement provides a route for administering fluid, blood, and medication. An IO line is as efficient as an intravenous route and can be inserted quickly, even in the most poorly perfused patients. http://emedicine.medscape.com/article/908610-overview

Gastrostomy Feeding Tube—A feeding tube is a tube that is inserted into your stomach through your abdomen. The tube is used to supply nutrition when you have trouble eating. The procedure of inserting the tube is called by various names including percutaneous endoscopic gastrostomy (PEC), esophagogastroduodenoscopy (EGD), and G-tube insertion. This treatment is used for people who have trouble eating on their own ... This is also for individuals who can eat but aren't getting enough nutrition or fluids orally. The feeding tube can also be used to administer medications. http://www.healthline.com/health/feeding-tube-insertion-gastrostomy#Overview1

Lennox-Gastaut Syndrome—Lennox-Gastaut syndrome is a severe form of epilepsy. Seizures usually begin before 4 years of age. Most children with Lennox-Gastaut syndrome experience some degree of impaired intellectual functioning or information processing, along with developmental delays, and behavioral disturbances. Lennox-Gastaut syndrome can be caused by brain malformations, perinatal asphyxia, severe head injury, central nervous system infection and inherited degenerative or metabolic conditions. In 30-35 percent of cases, no cause can be found. http://www.ninds.nih.gov/disorders/lennoxgastautsyndrome/lennoxgastautsyndrome.htm

Multiple Sclerosis—Multiple sclerosis (MS) is an unpredictable, often disabling disease of the central nervous system that disrupts the flow of information within the brain, and between the brain and body. http://www.nationalmssociety.org/What-is-MS

Petechaie—Petechiae (pronounced puh-TEE-kee-ee) are pinpoint, round spots that appear on the skin as a result of bleeding under the skin. The bleeding causes the petechiae to appear red, brown or purple. Petechiae commonly appear in clusters and may look like a rash. Petechiae may indicate a number of conditions, ranging from minor blood vessel injuries to life-threatening medical conditions. http://www.mayoclinic.org/symptoms/petechiae/basics/definition/sym-20050724.

Posturing, in brain injury—Decorticate posture is an abnormal posturing that involves rigidity, flexion of the arms, clenched fists, and extended legs (held out straight). The arms are bent inward toward the body with the wrists and fingers bent and held on the chest. This type of posturing is a sign of severe damage to the brain. It requires immediate medical attention. http://www.mybwmc.org/library/1/003300

Progressive Supranuclear Palsy—Progressive supranuclear palsy (PSP) is a neurodegenerative brain disease that has no known cause, treatment or cure. It affects nerve cells that control walking, balance, mobility, vision, speech, and swallowing. Five to six people per 100,000 will develop PSP. Symptoms begin, on average, when an individual is in the early 60's, but may start as early as in the 40's. PSP is slightly more common in men than women, but PSP has no known geographical, occupational or racial preference. http://www.psp.org/education/

TPN—Total parenteral (pronounced pa-**ren**-ter-ull) nutrition is often referred to as TPN for short. TPN is intravenous or IV nutrition. This means that if your child is on TPN, he or she is getting all of his or her nutrition – total nutrition – intravenously or through an IV. http://www.chp.edu/CHP/faq+about+tpn+intestine

VNS—Vagus nerve stimulation (VNS) may prevent or lessen seizures by sending regular, mild pulses of electrical energy to the brain via the vagus nerve. https://www.epilepsy.com/learn/treating-seizures-and-epilepsy/devices/vagus-nerve-stimulation-vns.